IN SEARCH OF A FATHER

James Robison

IN SEARCH OF A FATHER

LIFE'S ANSWER SERIES

Tyndale House
Publishers, Inc.
Wheaton, Illinois

Library of Congress
Catalog Card Number 79-66817
ISBN 0-8423-1634-5, paper
Copyright © 1980 by James Robison
All rights reserved
First printing, March 1980
Printed in the United States of America

CONTENTS

PART ONE: GOD AND FATHERHOOD

1 WHO NEEDS A FATHER? 9

2 ABANDONED FATHERHOOD 15

3 OUR HEAVENLY FATHER 26

4 THE FATHER WHO NEVER FAILS 38

PART TWO: GOD AND CHILD DEVELOPMENT

5 FATHERHOOD: A CHANNEL OF LOVE 51

6 RAISING CONFIDENT CHILDREN 60

7 TO DISCIPLINE WITH LOVE 70

8 CHILDREN AND SEX ROLES 74

9 HELPING CHILDREN GROW 81

PART THREE: GOD AND HIS FAMILY

10 PROCLAIMING GOD AS FATHER 97

11 A NEW FAMILY AND FUTURE 108

PART ONE

GOD AND FATHERHOOD

1

WHO NEEDS A FATHER?

On November 18, 1978, only a few days before Thanksgiving, Americans were shocked by the most bizarre tragedy ever to stain the pages of their religious history. U. S. Representative Leo Ryan of California, who had been investigating the suspicious activities of an American cult living on a farming commune in Guyana, was slain as he boarded an airplane to leave the settlement. Members of a television news crew who had accompanied the congressman were massacred along with him. Immediately afterwards, Jim Jones, the cult leader, and more than 900 of his followers committed suicide, most of them by gulping a grape-flavored soft drink spiked with cyanide.

Why? The question echoed in millions of minds around the world. Why would so many people place such gullible faith in a man like Jim Jones, an unstable and egotistical individual? Why would hundreds display such fanatical loyalty as that demonstrated by mothers who at Jones' command pried open the mouths of their babies, forced the deadly liquid down their throats, then watched as the children writhed and screamed in agony?

I believe God gives us the answer to that question. He has been giving us the answer for a long time, but America hasn't been listening. America has rather tuned in to its learned intellectuals, its atheistic philosophers, and its secular sociologists.

Ironically, now that social catastrophe stands at the

door, even the philosophers and sociologists are seeing that human beings have a basic need for love, both as individuals and as a society. That need can be fulfilled in its totality through: a father, a family, a future.

In his Word, God identifies these needs through his commandments. Because God wants the best for us, because he wants us to reach the full potential he envisioned for us when he created us, he commands us to do the very things that will fulfill our basic needs.

In his Word, he commands us to recognize the authority of our natural fathers (and mothers too). Specifically, we need a person in our lives who exercises authority and provides the masculine roles that only a father can fulfill.

God commands us to establish families and to live in those families in loving service to one another, providing for one another's needs.

God commands us to look forward to the future, an exciting future in which he guarantees joy and fulfillment if we believe in him and accept his Son, Jesus Christ, as Lord and Savior.

In America, the family is falling apart. "Family" is sociologically defined as "two or more people related by bonds of marriage or blood, sharing a common residence." Normally we think of the family as consisting of a husband and wife (father and mother) and children. Not many years ago, that was the only group spoken of as a family.

Today we hear about all kinds of alternatives to the traditional family. As divorce becomes commonplace and as premarital and extramarital sex and homosexuality increase, many young people are growing up without fathers, without any true family background, and without any sense of security concerning their identity, their purpose in life, or their future.

This helps explain why a Jim Jones can pose as a prophet, call himself God, and find hundreds who are unstable enough to believe in him. It explains how such a man, himself rootless and insecure, can put together a window display of caring and find unloved hundreds who will do his every bidding without question.

Jim Jones gave his deceived followers a father image they had never had before. He gave them a family, promising them that they would live together, work together, and die together. He gave them a future, however false it was. He said, "We're going to a better land; we'll see each other there." And because they were so starved for purpose and hope, they believed him. They trusted a counterfeit.

In his book *The Role of the Father in Child Development*, sociologist Michael Lamb said, "It is difficult to escape the implication (seen in a number of scientific studies) that the enduring relationships within the family system are ideal and that, if this system is to be replaced, the alternatives are unlikely to be as simple as often implied."

The Guyana incident offers a mortifying illustration of the tragic results the "alternatives" are capable of producing. Nor should anyone be lulled into thinking the Jim Jones incident is an anomaly that proves nothing. Weird sects and false prophets are flourishing as America rejects God and his church, as the family disintegrates and the nation is left fatherless.

God has maintained from the beginning—and sociologists now are beginning to realize—that the family unit is the essential building block of civilized society. The family is where children become socialized; i.e., that is where they learn how to interact on an intimate basis with other people. They learn about love and purpose and the meaning of life. They learn what is expected of them, both by other family members and by the world around them. They form their basic concepts about themselves and their potential and develop their fundamental personality traits. Ideally the family is where they learn about God's love and mercy and their accountability to him.

Without a proper family environment, sociologists have discovered, children don't acquire these basic concepts and behavior patterns. They don't become properly socialized.

Jim Jones' People's Temple and the plethora of other cults illustrate what happens when children don't have the kind of family lives God intended them to have. Most people who join such cults are frustrated, rootless people, people who feel rejected, who feel their interests have been overlooked and that their lives are of no value to society. Many are young people without strong family ties who have not been able to handle life's problems. They are searching for a strong, dynamic leader or movement that could give them instant solutions. Not only are they socially mobile, having severed whatever ties they might have had with the mainstream of society, but they are also in psychological transition. They are looking for something—their identity, their purpose, their niche in life.

A survivor of the People's Temple explained his involvement to an Associated Press reporter: "After I got out of the Marine Corps, basically I was wandering around, taking odd jobs, living off unemployment. I wanted to do something in my life where I felt I was helping people and doing something constructive in the social sense."

When young people reach adulthood without knowing their purpose for living, they are easy prey for those who want to use them for their own purposes. Wanderers looking for a cause had better beware. No matter how noble their intentions, they are leaving themselves open to the trickery of Satan, who has all sorts of causes to offer them.

Perhaps one good thing about the disintegration of the family in American life is that it has brought the importance of the father in the family to the attention of the social scientists.

Traditionally, the father has come to be regarded primarily as the provider. He has received little credit for the upbringing of the children. Since the father has been outside the home for most of the day, while the mother has spent most of her day with the children, it has been assumed that the mother played the most important role in determining how the children turned out. These assumptions have given birth to matriarchal slogans such as "The hand that rocks the cradle rules the world."

However, with so many marriages breaking up and with custody of the children so often going to the mother, sociologists have recently put greater focus on the effects fatherlessness can have on children. They are learning that the child without a father is dangerously deprived of impressions and influences vital to his or her proper development.

Recognizing the rapid increase in father-absent homes, sociologist Dennis Meredith surveyed numerous biographies of famous people. In his book *Father Power* (co-authored with Henry Biller) he summarizes that research. Those who had made a lasting imprint on their world, through constructive achievement, had grown up in a warm, encouraging family with both parents in the home.

Social scientists who have delved into the role of the father in the family unit have produced information that further explains Meredith's discovery. Basically, their studies have turned up evidence that the father in some ways contributes more to the socialization of children than the mother. Though the mother spends more time with the child, much of that time is devoted to "caring" activities—bathing, feeding, dressing, etc. The activities of the father with the child are more likely to be of the type that contributes to the child's social development.

Those activities and how they influence sons and daughters, despite the relatively little time most fathers have with their children, will be discussed in more detail in later chapters. Let it suffice to say at this point that the father's role determines in large degree the child's emotional and intellectual development, creativity, sense of security, motivation to achieve, sense of moral values, and ability to relate to other people and to the world. The father's part is also found to be crucial in sex-role adoption, a most important discovery in view of the alarming increase of homosexuality in American society.

2

ABANDONED FATHERHOOD

One of the most important roles of the father in the home is his role as an authority figure. The father has traditionally been the one who has had the last word, or at least the one with the most power to enforce the last word. He has been a parent exerting firm discipline, insisting on obedience and respect.

God never intended children to grow up without a father image in the home. In Genesis 2:24 he commanded: "Therefore shall a man leave his father and his mother, and shall cleave unto his wife: and they shall be one flesh."

This commandment lays the groundwork for a permanent union between a man and his wife. One result of such permanence is that the father will remain in the home when children arrive, and that he will be a father to them.

The parental authority vested in the father is seen in the familiar Old Testament story of Joseph being sold into slavery by his brothers. His brothers came to him later, after he had risen to a position of great power in Egypt, because a famine had struck their land and they wanted to buy grain from him. When Jacob died, they were afraid of possible reprisal by Joseph. So they sent a messenger to him: "Thy father did command before he died, saying, So shall ye say unto Joseph, Forgive, I pray thee now, the trespass of thy brethren, and their sin; for they did unto thee evil: and now, we pray thee, forgive the trespass of the servants of the God of thy father" (Genesis 50:16, 17).

Obviously the brothers expected the supposed command of their father to be as binding on Joseph after his death as it would have been if he were alive. And Joseph took it that way as well.

God meant for the father, the head of the household, to be a person of just such power and authority. He intended the father to be so respected and honored in life that his children would obey his commands even after his death.

The Lord vested such authority in the father for a twofold purpose.

First, God in his infinite wisdom was not unaware of what sociologists are discovering in twentieth-century America. He knew quite well the importance of the father in the socialization of children. He knew that children who don't learn how to be responsible people become both a liability and a threat to society. God planned an orderly society, one in which he could reveal himself, and he recognized that such a society could exist only if children grow up with a wholesome respect for authority, a respect primarily learned through their relationship with their father.

This truth is borne out repeatedly in the Scriptures, but it's presented most graphically in Proverbs. The writers of this book repeatedly emphasize the role of the father in the development of the child:

> *My son, hear the instruction of thy father, and forsake not the law of thy mother. Proverbs 1:8*
>
> *Hear, ye children, the instruction of a father, and attend to know understanding. Proverbs 4:1*
>
> *Hearken unto thy father that begat thee, and despise not thy mother when she is old. Proverbs 23:22*

> *Train up a child in the way he should go: and when he is old, he will not depart from it.*
> Proverbs 22:6

God placed the father in the home and entrusted to him the major role in "training up the child." In his law and his instructions to his people, he provided for those who became fatherless through death or separation (as we shall see in greater detail later). God knew the importance of the father in the socialization of children.

Secondly, God chose the father to be his instrument in revealing himself to each succeeding generation of humanity.

God chose Abram to be the father of a great nation. He promised to bless him and to make him a blessing to "all families of the earth" (Genesis 12:1-3). After that, when God spoke to Abram's descendants he identified himself as the God of their fathers.

> *And the Lord appeared unto him [Isaac] the same night, and said, I am the God of Abraham thy father. . . .* Genesis 26:24
> *And Jacob said, O God of my father Abraham, and God of my father Isaac, the Lord which saidst unto me . . .* Genesis 32:9
> *Moreover he [God] said [to Moses], I am the God of thy father, the God of Abraham, the God of Isaac, and the God of Jacob. . . .* Exodus 3:6

In setting up the family, and establishing the father as the head of the family, God was not merely forming a training unit for society. He was creating a repository for his Word, a classroom through which successive generations of people would be taught about him. His intention in this regard is clearly stated in Deuteronomy 11:18-21:

> Therefore shall ye lay up these my words in your heart and in your soul, and bind them for a sign upon your hand, that they may be as frontlets between your eyes. And ye shall teach them your children, speaking of them when thou sittest in thine house, and when thou walkest by the way, when thou liest down and when thou risest up. And thou shalt write them upon the door posts of thine house, and upon thy gates: That your days may be multiplied, and the days of your children, in the land which the Lord sware unto your fathers to give them, as the days of heaven upon the earth.

This is God's design for the family and for the role of the father in the home. He promised that if fathers (and mothers) would follow his plan and accept the responsibilities he entrusted to them, they would have long, fulfilling lives, and so would their children. Their days would be like "heaven upon earth."

You don't have to be a sociologist to realize that the family system in America today is not following God's design. You don't have to make a scientific study to discover that fathers are not fulfilling their responsibilities in the home. All you have to do to understand how far the American family and the American father have drifted from God's plan is to look at the results. In other words, look at the children. Look at the young people of America as they come out of father-absent or father-deficient homes and consider how they are turning out.

Do America's young people enjoy long, fulfilling lives? Are their days like heaven on earth?

Suicide is a leading cause of death among young people. Many are so unhappy that they not only do not live long lives, but actually take steps to shorten their lifespan.

Morally, our nation wallows in bankruptcy. Many of the marriages that are failing do so because young people grew up without acquiring God-given values and standards. They don't know the meaning of sexual fidelity and true, permanent commitment to a single marital partner. Too many of them have experienced sex before marriage, usually with more than one person. According to one recent survey, over half of America's fifteen to nineteen-year-old girls admitted participation in premarital sex. Also, homosexuality is a widespread, militant force in the country.

Lacking purpose and values to guide their lives, young people continue to turn to drugs and alcohol. The so-called "drug scare" has faded, not because kids have stopped using drugs but because their parents have become more resigned to it and because society has become more accepting toward it. While drug abuse is still a serious problem, however, alcohol abuse has quietly become a problem of much greater concern. Official estimates place the number of "problem drinkers" among young people under eighteen at about 1.3 million. More than six million teenagers are believed to be using alcohol, and the age at which youngsters begin to drink is lowering every year.

Crime flourishes, especially crimes of violence. Some of our social theorists still hold to the belief that poverty causes crime. But that belief is becoming more and more difficult to defend as evidence increases that material wants and needs have little to do with the kind of crime wave this country is experiencing. Young people from prosperous, middle-class homes and even wealthy families are involved in crime as well as poor children of the inner cities.

Family failure and father failure are nowhere more glaringly displayed than in the statistics on child abuse and abortion. For many children, home is a hell on earth. Children not only are neglected and unloved, but actually brutalized and exploited. In the case of abortion, the child isn't even allowed to enter the world alive. Yet in America this killing of the unborn has become an accepted alternative to responsible parenthood. It has even become an official policy of our national government through rulings handed down by the Supreme Court and legislation granting financial aid to pregnant women who can't afford to pay for the murder of their own babies.

Broken homes and father-absent and father-deficient homes are the major contributors to all of these ills. A marked relationship has been found between father deprivation and crimes of theft and personal violence, such as murder, rape, and aggravated assault.

The sickening consequences of the breakdown of the family and the father image are written in the misery and death of our children, and in the blood of the innocent victims of their desperation.

The consequences are also to be read in the spiritual chaos besetting the nation. As surely as the abandonment of God's design for the family and parenthood wreaks havoc on society, it also disrupts his plan for revealing himself and his truth to succeeding generations.

The father in the home should give the child his first conception of what God is like. By observing his father as he fulfills his role in the family, the child should be able to see the role God desires to fulfill to perfection in his life, and for eternity. The loss of that father image closes a curtain between the child's mind and an understanding of God as a loving Father. That curtain, thank God, can be parted, but in many young lives that never happens. Instead, the disoriented young person often turns to drugs, alcohol, sexual perversion, or false messiahs in search of the meaning and purpose he or she fails to find in the home.

Author-philosopher William F. Buckley, Jr., in what has to be the understatement of the century, said the Guyana incident "shows an insufficiency of spiritual reserves" in America. In fact, it shows the spiritual calamity that reigns when the family falls apart and fathers no longer shoulder their God-given responsibilities, leading people to misplaced trust in a false father figure.

When a nation turns its back on God's way, it becomes a "perverse and crooked generation" (Deuteronomy 32:5). It becomes a nation "void of counsel, neither is there any understanding in them" (Deuteronomy 32:28). The children of such a nation are easy prey for false prophets who come dressed in sheep's clothing, but inwardly are "ravening wolves" who want only to devour them (Matthew 7:15). Jim Jones is not the only example of such false prophets. Before him there was Charles Manson, who so captivated more than two dozen young people that they obeyed his instructions to commit brutal murder. There was also Dean Corll, who lured young drifters into his lair where he committed homosexual rape against them and then killed and buried some twenty-seven of them in Houston, Texas.

There are hundreds of false leaders and cults disseminating untrue doctrines and luring thousands of bewildered young people into spiritual dungeons—the Hare Krishna, Sun Myung Moon's Unification church, Scientology, the Children of God, to name a few of the most notorious ones.

When marriages dissolve or when fathers leave the home or abdicate their positions of responsibility or abuse and misuse their authority in the home, they offer their children up as living sacrifices to these wolves. All false prophets who teach false doctrines and all of the sects and cults that entrap bewildered, fatherless people with their counterfeit demonstrations of love and empty promises are "ravening wolves." They exploit the troubled and the helpless for their own selfish purposes.

Though the problem has become especially severe in modern America, father-absence and father-deficiency is by no means a new problem. It has existed in varying degrees down through the ages. It even manifested itself rather dramatically in several incidents recorded in the Bible.

One noteworthy example of father-deficiency can be gleaned from the calling of Abram. Genesis 12:1 documents the call in these words. "Now the Lord had said unto Abram, Get thee out of thy country, and from thy kindred, and from thy father's house, unto a land that I will shew thee."

Why did God command Abram (later to be renamed Abraham, which means "father") to leave his father's house? In Joshua 24:2 we read: "And Joshua said unto all the people, Thus saith the Lord God of Israel, Your fathers dwelt on the other side of the flood in old time, even Terah, the father of Abraham, and the father of Nachor: and they served other gods."

The father of Abraham, the man God chose to head the family of faith through whom he would reveal himself to mankind, "served other gods." God had to remove Abraham from the influence of an idolatrous family before he could use him for the purpose he ordained for him.

Abraham's case doesn't stand alone. Repeatedly, God had to abandon fathers who failed to fulfill their responsibilites and then work through others. The Lord reminds the nation Israel of this dismal fact in Jeremiah 34:12-14:

> Therefore the word of the Lord came to Jeremiah from the Lord, saying, Thus saith the Lord, the God of Israel; I made a covenant with your fathers in the day that I brought them forth out of the land of Egypt, out of the house of bondmen . . . but your fathers hearkened not unto me, neither inclined their ear.

Jesus indicted the fathers of Israel even more severely in Matthew 23:30-32, when he said to the scribes and Pharisees:

> And [you] say, If we had been in the days of our fathers, we would not have been partakers with them in the blood of the prophets. Wherefore ye be witnesses unto yourselves, that ye are the children of them which killed the prophets. Fill [or finish] ye up then the measure of your fathers.

The Bible also paints a most disturbing picture of the consequences of father-failure in Exodus 20:5— "I the Lord thy God am a jealous God, visiting the iniquity of the fathers upon the children unto the third and fourth generation of them that hate me."

The warning is plain enough: When fathers turn their backs on God, their nation can spend a long time getting back into fellowship with the Lord and in a position to receive his blessings.

God knew that earthly fathers would often fail to live up to his expectations for them. That's why he commanded Israel to attend to the fatherless: "Ye shall not afflict any widow, or fatherless child" (Exodus 22:22). "And the Levite, (because he hath no part nor inheritance with thee) and the stranger, and the fatherless, and the widow, which are within thy gates, shall come, and shall eat and be satisfied, that the Lord thy God may bless thee in all the work of thine hand which thou doest" (Deuteronomy 14:29).

In some instances, God made special instruments of those who had been taken from their father or who had been taken and reared by someone other than their natural father. The story of Esther stands as one example:

"[Mordecai] brought up Hadassah, that is, Esther, his uncle's daughter: for she had neither father nor mother, and the maid was fair and beautiful; whom Mordecai, when her father and mother were dead, took for his own daughter."

So if the immediate family failed, for whatever reason, God turned to other relatives and to the community as a whole to provide fathers for the fatherless.

However, he went even further. If the family and the community both failed, God himself stepped into the breach. He intervened spiritually.

It is not the nature of a just and loving God to punish one person for the sins of another. He makes it plain, through his Word, that this is not his intent: "The soul that sinneth, it shall die. The son shall not bear the iniquity of the father, neither shall the father bear the iniquity of the son: the righteousness of the righteous shall be upon him, and the wickedness of the wicked shall be upon him" (Ezekiel 18:20).

Certainly, it would be far better for the children of America if their fathers would fulfill their responsibilities and teach their children about God and lead them to a saving knowledge of Jesus Christ. But a child is not hopelessly lost if he or she has a father who fails to do so. It would be far better for father-absent or father-deficient children if their relatives or the community as a whole would take charge and provide them with the fathering they need. But children are not hopelessly lost even when their families and their society fail to come through for them.

Thank God, he himself intervenes in the lives of those who turn to him. He sees to it that they have a father—the Heavenly Father. He brings them into a family—his own family. He gives them a future—an eternal future, where they find complete fulfillment in fellowship with him and with other believers.

In Psalm 10:14, God describes himself as "helper of the fatherless." What a helper he is to those who allow him to become their Father!

3

OUR HEAVENLY FATHER

Let me tell you a story from contemporary life that illustrates what it means to have God as your Father.

A woman wandered down the streets of Houston, Texas, one night, a baby in her womb. It was time for the baby to be born, but she didn't know how she could care for her child because his alcoholic father had deserted her.

She walked into the ward of a charity hospital and gave birth to her baby, a boy. Since the boy had no father, she put an ad in the newspaper asking someone to take the baby and care for him.

The newspaper ad was answered by a Houston couple. They took the baby, loved him, and cared for him for five years.

At that time, the boy's mother decided she could care for her son. She got him from the couple who had been raising him and took him with her to another city. The boy would spend the next ten years with his mother, but they would be tragic, turbulent years.

The mother married a man who couldn't read or write. He hardly provided a wholesome father model for the young boy in the home.

Did I say home? They moved so many times the boy became confused about the meaning of the word. They were so poor that none of the houses they lived in could have been properly described as a home, even if they could have remained in one for any appreciable length of time.

The marriage to the illiterate man was a stormy affair, and the boy saw little warmth or husband-wife affection demonstrated by his mother and stepfather. The marriage soon ended in divorce.

Having been first fatherless, then reared briefly by a father substitute, then subjected to a strongly negative father influence, the boy had now come full circle. He was fatherless again.

He might have been better off had he remained so.

His mother married the man who had been the boy's real father, an alcoholic. This father brought fires of hell into the home and into the life of the boy.

The father often came home raging drunk. He would curse the boy and the boy's mother. He would become violent. On one occasion he seized the boy's mother by the throat and choked her until she lost consciousness and fell to the floor.

A few days after the choking incident, the father came home again drunk, and said, "I'm going to kill you." Had the mother not fainted, the father almost certainly would have killed her, but in his drunken stupor he thought she was dead. He looked at the boy and said, "I'm going to kill you too."

The boy ran into another part of the house, found a gun, and pointed it at his father. "If you so much as move one hand, I'll shoot you," the boy said.

Hatred so throbbed in the boy's heart and fear so dominated his panic-stricken soul that had his father so much as lifted his hand to his cheek the boy would have squeezed the trigger on the rifle and blown his own father into eternity.

The father didn't move, but just stood there cursing the boy. He cursed so loudly and so long that the neighbors heard him and called the police. The police came and took the boy's father away.

The child's life was a shambles. With his background and his home environment, most sociologists would say he had no chance to become properly oriented and go on to useful, productive life. They would look at a case like his and say this boy was almost certain to become an alcoholic, drug addict, or criminal. They would say that boys with such unstable home lives sometimes even become homosexuals or rapists.

One night, however, the boy had the privilege of being in the company of some genuine Christians, people who knew and loved the Lord. He had joined a church when he was younger, just because he had said he would like to go to Heaven and the preacher had said that all he had to do was be christened. The christening hadn't worked, though. It had brought no change in the boy's life. It had only made him a hypocrite.

On this particular night, however, a pastor was conducting an evangelistic service. He said he wasn't going to preach a sermon, that he simply wanted his teenagers to stand and tell what Jesus meant to them. One after another, young people stood up, their faces glowing, and said, "Jesus is real to me," or "He lives in my life."

Soon the boy began to cry. Finally the pastor said, "If you would like to receive the Jesus who changed these young people's lives, if you would like to know the Father, come and take my hand."

The boy reached out and grabbed the back of the chair in front of him. He got to his feet, trembling and fighting the butterflies in his stomach.

When the preacher said, "Come," the boy knew in

his heart that he had never had a father. God said to his heart, "I want to be your Father."

He had never had a real family. God said to him, "I want to give you a family."

The boy still hesitated. He said in his heart, "If I do this, I don't know what will happen to me, I don't know where I will go next." God answered and said, "I want to establish your future, son—forever."

The boy felt afraid, but suddenly he was aware of someone coming toward him. He looked up and saw a lady, a preacher's wife. She held her glasses in one hand, her tears flowing so freely that she had to remove them. She put her other hand on the boy's shoulder and asked him, "Don't you want to go to Jesus? Don't you want to get right with God?"

The boy said, "Yes, but I'm afraid."

The woman said, "I'll go with you. Why don't we go together?"

He stepped into the aisle with that lady, walked down to the front, and put his hand in the preacher's hand. In that very moment he also put his life in God's hand.

That night God picked up an unwanted, unloved teenager—a boy who had no chance by this world's standards—and planted his feet on the Solid Rock.

A few years later, God spoke to the boy as a young man, filled his heart with boldness, and said, "I want you to preach." God sent that young man all over America, telling people about Jesus.

That unwanted baby, that desperate and love-deprived boy, that pitiful home environment—all of that, mixed with the grace of God—produced James Robison, the evangelist who is writing these words.

I was that little baby. I was that desperate, angry

young man. But I came to know the Father. I became one of the family—the family of God.

Investigators poking through the death scene after the mass suicide in Guyana found a tape recorder near the wooden chair Jim Jones had used as his pulpit and throne. When they played it, they heard babies crying, people screaming, and some of the cult leader's final instructions to his followers: "Mothers, you must keep your children under control. They must die with dignity."

God enables those who become his children to die with dignity, but more important, to live in victory!

Jim Jones's followers called him "Dad." But it goes without saying that God is a better father than Jim Jones or any other counterfeit messiah. In fact, God is superior to any human being as a father. To realize this, one has only to compare the attributes of God to those of natural fathers.

God is "The everlasting Father" (Isaiah 9:6).
Even the best human fathers serve only temporarily. They act as fathers only until their children reach adulthood. The major portion of the guidance and instruction they give must be administered within a period of about eighteen years. After that, they serve only in an advisory capacity. They no longer have close supervision over the development of their children; they have little control over their behavior. God actually planned it this way, because he ordained that a man should "leave his father and his mother" (Genesis 2:24) when he became mature enough to marry and begin his own family.

But God continues to be a Father throughout life in this world and on into eternity to those who are born spiritually into his family.

God is all-powerful.
What earthly father hasn't looked lovingly upon a son or daughter and said to himself, "How I wish I could do such and such for you! If only I had the strength, if only I had the resources, I would do this thing for you, my child."

God has no limitations. Whatever he wills to do, he has power to do. With God, nothing is impossible (Luke 1:37).

God is all-knowing.
First John 3:20 proclaims the important truth that "God . . . knoweth all things."

Earthly fathers, despite their limitations, are able to do many things for their offspring. However, with their incomplete understanding, they don't always know what's best for their children. Because he knows all things, God knows the right thing to do for his children, and always does what's best.

Children often have to beg their earthly fathers for the things they need. They have to argue and convince their earthly fathers before these mere mortals see and understand the need and act to meet it.

God, on the other hand, is aware of the needs of his children even before they ask (Matthew 6:8). His knowledge of all things, combined with his ability to do anything, guarantees that all of his children's needs will be properly met.

God is an ever-present Father.
Even during the eighteen years, more or less, that a child is ideally in the home with his earthly father, he is actually in the presence of that father for only a few hours a day. During those few hours, he has his father's attention only briefly. One study indicates that American fathers who remain with their families

spend an average of only twenty minutes a day doing something with their children.

God never leaves his children (Hebrews 13:5). He is constantly present with them, and they have his undivided attention every minute of their lives. His thoughts toward his children are more numerous than the grains of sand that cover the earth (Psalm 139:17, 18). A child does relatively few things with his natural father. Everything a child of God does he does with his Father.

God is a spiritual Father.
The Bible tells us that "God is a Spirit" (John 4:24). That fact is far more important than it might seem.

In their fleshly form, human fathers labor under the limitations imposed by their physical bodies and finite minds. In serving as fathers, they are encumbered by the burden of their own needs and restricted by their own frailties. They can't devote all their time and energy to meeting the needs of their children because they have their own to contend with.

Being in essence spirit, God knows no such limitations and restrictions. He is unencumbered by human needs and frailties. He can devote all his time to ministering to the needs of his children.

God is a truth-revealing Father.
However much an earthly father might wish to reveal pure truth to his children in instructing them, he is hampered by his human fallibility. On the other hand, God can (and does) reveal pure truth to his children.

When Peter told Jesus that he was the Christ, Jesus said, "Flesh and blood hath not revealed it unto thee, but my Father which is in heaven" (Matthew 16:17).

Jesus said, in Luke 10:21, that his Father, Lord of

32

Heaven, had hid certain truths from the wise and prudent, but had revealed them unto babes—his children.

In John 5:19 Jesus disclosed that even the truths he knew were revealed to him by his heavenly Father. "The Son can do nothing of himself, but what he seeth the Father do."

God is a perfect protector.
Natural fathers, because of all their limitations, have neither the power nor the wisdom to protect their children from all the physical dangers and harmful influences that threaten them. Jesus informs us that the Heavenly Father never fails as a protector. Warning those who would despise little children that come to God, Jesus said, "Take heed that ye despise not one of these little ones; for I say unto you, That in heaven their angels do always behold the face of my Father which is in heaven" (Matthew 18:10).

God is a loving and concerned Father.
Many earthly fathers find it hard to be gentle and loving with their children. Through the macho idea the world has instilled in them concerning what it means to be "a man," they never learn to express affection, to let their children know they really care about them.

The Heavenly Father unabashedly expresses his love for his children. "Jesus loves me, this I know" may be a children's Sunday school song, but its message has sustained sailors in the stormiest seas, soldiers in the bloodiest battles, and mothers in the pain of childbirth and the agony of losing a baby to the grave. The best known verse in the Bible expresses God's love for every human being: "For God so loved

33

the world, that he gave his only begotten Son, that whosoever believeth in him should not perish, but have everlasting life" (John 3:16).

Sometimes natural fathers have a hard time showing love for their children because of the children's behavior. A father whose child has disappointed him time and again or has caused the family shame and grief may in effect disown that child. The love of God the Father, on the other hand, is everlasting. It doesn't depend on perfection on the part of the child, because God loved the child even before the child knew he had God as his Father.

"God commendeth [demonstrates] his love toward us, in that, while we were yet sinners, Christ died for us" (Romans 5:8).

God loved us so much that even while we were in a completely hopeless condition of sinfulness, while we were his enemies, he made the supreme sacrifice of sending Jesus to the cross for us so he could redeem us from our sins.

In 1 Peter 5:7, God is revealed as one so concerned for his children that he wants them to bring every problem and anxiety they have to him: "Casting all your care upon him, for he careth for you."

God the Father loves his children so intensely that he doesn't want them to exhaust themselves trying to cope with the burdens and difficulties of everyday life. He pleads with them to bring those burdens to him and let him carry the load, so they will be free to enjoy life in all its abundance.

God is a merciful and understanding Father.
Some children go through life never experiencing the approval and acceptance of their natural fathers. Earthly fathers can be judgmental, demanding, stub-

born, insensitive, and imperceptive. Even the best of them often tend to expect too much of their offspring.

In his Word, God reveals himself as a Father who forgives his children for their wrongdoing. His mercy is "from everlasting to everlasting" (Psalm 103:17). He also reveals himself as a wise Father who makes allowances for his children's weaknesses. "Like a father pitieth his children, so the Lord pitieth them that fear him. For he knoweth our frame; he remembereth that we are dust" (Psalm 103:13, 14).

God is an unfailing provider.
"Seek ye first the kingdom of God, and his righteousness," Jesus said, "and all these things shall be added unto you" (Matthew 6:33).

The words "all these things" referred to the material needs that men concern themselves with—food, clothing, housing. The words of a hymn Christians often sing at Thanksgiving come to mind: "God, our Maker, doth provide, for our wants to be supplied." He provides so bountifully that we can be free to give generously and cheerfully. This was Paul's thought when he wrote to the Philippians, thanking them for sending him gifts in a time of need. He said: "But my God shall supply all your need according to his riches in glory by Christ Jesus" (Philippians 4:19).

Jesus in many instances stressed the superiority of the Heavenly Father over natural fathers. Verses illustrating this point sprinkle the pages of the Gospels.

"Love your enemies, bless those who curse you...," Jesus said in the Sermon on the Mount. Why? ". . . That ye may be children of your Father which is in heaven" (Matthew 5:44, 45).

Jesus implied that as children of your natural father

you love only relatives and friends. To be children of the Heavenly Father requires more. It requires loving even enemies and those who hate you. The reason is that the Heavenly Father's character is superior to your earthly father's and therefore demands superior conduct from his children.

In one of the most dramatic incidents recorded in the New Testament, Jesus revealed God the Father to be so far superior to any earthly father that comparing the two seems ridiculous. Jesus and his disciples were in a boat on the Sea of Galilee when a vicious storm arose. The disciples rebuked the Lord because he slept in the stern of the buffeted vessel, seemingly unconcerned about their danger. Jesus, in turn, rebuked them. "Ye of little faith," he said, meaning, "you who don't depend fearlessly on the love and power of God, you who don't recognize the sovereignty of your Heavenly Father over all things." Then he rebuked the wind and the sea, and the Scripture says the ferocious elements lapsed into a "great calm."

Then, it is reported, the disciples marveled, saying, "What manner of man is this, that even the winds and the sea obey him" (Matthew 8:23-27).

He was that manner of man who has the Heavenly Father as his Father. Such a man is the child of the King who controls all. There are things that earthly fathers can't do for their children, however much they might want to, simply because there are forces and situations they don't have the ability to control. But no force or ability is beyond God the Father's control. Even the wind and the sea obey him.

God the Father is so far superior to any earthly father that Jesus says only God is worthy to be called Father. "And call no man your father upon the earth: for one is your Father, which is in heaven."

He was speaking to a people who had strong family ties. In Judea, many fathers strove diligently to fulfill their parental obligations to their children. In that culture the father figure remained clear and sturdy. Yet Jesus said, in effect, "God is so far above any human being that it's an insult to him to use the name 'father' in reference to even the best earthly fathers."

God is everything anyone could ever want or hope for in a father, a better Father than any human mind could ever imagine.

4

THE FATHER WHO NEVER FAILS

When the roles of the father in child development are considered in detail, the need of every child to know God as Father becomes painfully evident.

Many sociological studies report that the quality of relationship between the father and the child are more important than the specific techniques used in dealing with the child. Nevertheless, in our society debate rages over techniques—which are best, which are most effective. Those who know God as Father realize, however, that quality is indeed the more important element. The quality of a genuine personal relationship with the Heavenly Father assures us that God will never fail to fulfill his fatherly roles. We should imitate this in our relationship with our children.

The prime ingredients of effective fathering, it has been found, are:

(1) Sensory awareness—the father's ability to perceive that he is like the child in many ways, and vice versa.

(2) The ability to receive fulfillment through the child's performance.

(3) The ability to exert general physical control over the child's development.

The Heavenly Father surely perceives he is like his children, since he created them in his image.

He receives fulfillment in the performance of his children, as the Scriptures inform us in many passages. He regards those who believe in him as his inheritance (Ephesians 1:18), and he is pleased when his children demonstrate faithfulness and obedience.

Experts on fathering know the importance of examining one's own father in determining what a father should be like.

When God is your Father, that investigation always produces gratifying results. What better father image could anyone have than that projected by the loving, caring, all-powerful, all-wise God of the universe? God the Father always uses his unlimited resources in the most constructive ways for the benefit of his children. He makes correct decisions on every matter. He sets the proper limits on the child, allowing enough freedom for full development of potential, yet imposing enough restraint to ensure against reckless exploits that could impede or distort development.

Examining earthly fathers to gain insight into what fatherhood should or shouldn't be can be disastrous. It is, in fact, the documented cause of many of the social disasters we read about in the newspapers and hear about on television and radio every day. Natural fathers, in growing proportions, are failing miserably to fulfill their roles and to project the father image so vital to their children's development.

To give fathers their due, however, let me point out that almost overwhelming forces are working to increase the difficulty of their task. In modern society, fathers encounter special problems in fulfilling their role as provider and in coping with the ambiguity of roles they are expected to fill.

Adding immensely to both the burden and the confusion is the image of the father presented by communications and entertainment media. Family situations offered by television, for example, are almost always of a comic nature. They make no attempt to depict the father's role realistically. They often portray ambitious driving men, but seldom do they present family men as warm, successful fathers. As a result, boys get the impression as they grow up that a man can be either a vigorous, macho man or a warm, caring father, but not both.

With the father-image so blurred, fathers experience great frustration in defining and carrying out their roles. Not only that, but their children's respect for them is being undermined by the sharp contrast between the distorted media image and the real-life image projected by their fathers.

Finally, natural fathering is failing on an increasing scale because of the increase in divorces and subsequent remarriages. Sociological studies show that a succession of father models is unlikely to fill a child's psychological need for a father image, even if the models are individually satisfactory.

God the Father provides his children with a constant model. Not only does he give them the same Father throughout life, but a Father who is the same throughout life—in his character, attitudes, and conduct. These are qualities no human father could ever dream of matching.

GOD AS SIRE

One of the most significant contributions to American literature in the second half of this century is Alex Haley's novel, *Roots*. It ranks as one of the top bestsellers in history. A television drama series based on the story drew a bigger viewing audience than any program shown during the year it premiered except the Super Bowl football game.

Why such tremendous success in a population eighty percent white for a story that traced the history of a black family through the days of slavery and back to its origins in Africa?

I believe it is because America has become a rootless society. Blacks, with the complexities in family relationships brought on by the dehumanizing effects of slavery, are not alone in feeling disoriented and severed from their origins. With its great mobility and the downgrading of the past, American society as a whole has been shaken loose from its family tree.

Yet everyone has a tremendous psychological need to know where he "came from." Regardless of how much the existentialists may preach their "now generation" philosophies, human beings sense intuitively that where you come from has a lot to do with where you are now and where you are going.

Adrift from their ties with the past, Americans find themselves in the midst of a terrible identity crisis. Many young people fritter away years searching for answers to the questions "Who am I?" and "What am I doing here?"

The breakdown of marriage and the dissolution of the home in recent years has intensified this identity crisis. Many young people have been passed from parent to parent and household to household so often that they hardly even know their real father's name, much less his whereabouts or what he is like.

Having God as Father solves the identity crisis immediately. God reveals himself as spiritual sire to those who believe in him. He gives them his name. He identifies them, not only to themselves but to all the world, as his children.

Some might say, "Yes, but God 'sires' children only in the spiritual sense, and it doesn't mean as much to know your spiritual sire as it does to know your physical sire."

It should mean more. God makes it clear in his Word that spiritual birth is more important than physical birth though, of course, both are necessary.

The Bible makes much of the circumstances of the physical birth of Jesus, and God had good reason to do so. To be the sacrifice for our sins, Jesus had to be the sinless Son of God. He was literally sired by the Holy Spirit. He was the unique God-Man, the Diety incarnated and come to earth in human form.

Still, God reveals that Jesus' entrance into new life after his crucifixion and burial was in a sense a "birth" that consummated God's plan of redemption.

Writing about this, Paul says: "But God raised him [Jesus] from the dead. . . . And we declare unto you glad tidings, how that the promise which was made unto the fathers, God hath fulfilled the same unto us their children, in that he hath raised up Jesus again; as it is also written in the second psalm, Thou art my Son, this day have I begotten thee" (Acts 13:30-33).

The "promise" referred to is God's promise to make the descendants of Abraham a great nation through whom he would bless all peoples. Paul is saying this refers to a spiritual nation. It's not a nation that can trace its lineage in flesh and blood back to Abraham. Rather, it traces its lineage in faith—in belief in God— back to Abraham.

Jesus, Paul says, was "this day . . . begotten"—on the day of his resurrection—in a manner that is most important to the creation of this spiritual nation. He is saying that Jesus' being physically begotten would have been meaningless had he not also been spiritually begotten by being raised from the dead.

Paul expounds further on this theme in his epistle to the Colossians: "And he is the head of the body, the church: who is the beginning, the firstborn from the dead" (1:18).

In 1 Peter 1:3, God reveals to us that the Christian is begotten in the same way and at the same time as Jesus—that is, at the resurrection. "Blessed be the God and Father of our Lord Jesus Christ, which according to his abundant mercy hath begotten us again unto a lively hope by the resurrection of Jesus Christ from the dead."

The writer of Hebrews elaborates on the same theme: "For both he that sanctifieth [Jesus] and they who are sanctified are all of one: for which cause he is not ashamed to call them brethren, saying, I will declare thy name unto my brethren, in the midst of the church will I sing praise unto thee. And again, I will put my trust in him. And again, Behold I and the children which God hath given me" (2:11-13).

If you are a Christian, you are a brother of Jesus Christ. You are as much a part of the family of God as Jesus himself. You are a "joint-heir" with Christ (Romans 8:17). God has provided you all the credentials you need to establish your identity, your "roots," and your purpose in life.

God the Father shares with you:

His name: "Behold, what manner of love the Father hath bestowed upon us, that we should be called *the sons of God.* . . , Beloved, now are we the sons of God. . . ." (1 John 3:1, 2).

His nature: "Whereby are given unto us exceeding great and precious promises: that by these ye might be *partakers of the divine nature,* having escaped the corruption that is in the world through lust" (2 Peter 1:4).

His wealth: "According as his divine power *hath*

given unto us all things that pertain unto life and godliness, through the knowledge of him that hath called us to glory and virtue" (2 Peter 1:3). "Blessed be the God and Father of our Lord Jesus Christ, who *hath blessed us with all spiritual blessings* in heavenly places in Christ" (Ephesians 1:3).

His glory: "And when the chief Shepherd [Christ] shall appear, ye shall receive *a crown of glory* that fadeth not away" (1 Peter 5:4). "... That ye would walk worthy of God, who hath called you unto *his kingdom and glory*" (1 Thessalonians 2:12).

His future: "Surely goodness and mercy shall follow me all the days of my life: and *I will dwell in the house of the Lord for ever*" (Psalm 23:6).

Jesus, in his interview with Nicodemus, stressed the overwhelming importance of spiritual birth. "Except a man be born again [of the Spirit], he cannot see the kingdom of God," he said (John 3:3). No one can know God as Father and be part of God's family except by spiritual birth, the birth that comes through faith in Jesus Christ as Savior and Lord.

The Word of God makes it clear that without spiritual birth no life, in any meaningful sense, actually exists. In his dissertation following the account of the Lord's talk with Nicodemus, John the Baptist said: "He that believeth on the Son hath everlasting life: and he that believeth not the Son shall not see life; but the wrath of God abideth on him" (John 3:36).

Jesus also said, "Verily, verily, I say unto you, He that heareth my word, and believeth on him that sent me, hath everlasting life, and shall not come into condemnation; but is passed from death unto life" (John 5:24).

God fulfills to the utmost a Father role as sire, as name-giver, as link to both past and future.

No one born spiritually into the great family of God need ever suffer from an identity crisis or from confusion concerning origin or destiny. No earthly father could begin to give the assurance in these matters that the Heavenly Father provides his children.

GOD AS PROVIDER

Earthly fathers probably feel more stress and frustration in their role as provider for their children than in any other role they are called on to perform.

In modern society, the father's provider role is highly visible and overwhelmingly demanding. He is no longer the hunter, fisherman, or farmer working alone and in obscurity to gather food and fiber for the simple needs of his family. He must work with others. This necessity imposes on him the need to develop interpersonal skills—techniques in getting along with people—that fathers didn't need so acutely in primitive and agrarian societies. A father can be an excellent welder and yet fail as a provider by not being able to work with others.

As a hunter or farmer, a father might miss a shot at a deer or plow a crooked furrow without anyone's ever knowing it. Today's father is constantly under supervision by superiors who endlessly evaluate his job performance. No mistake that he makes escapes criticism, and even his best often is graded as not good enough.

Because of these conditions, many fathers become discouraged and drop out as providers. Others simply become victims of the ups, downs, and changes of a technological economy, joining, leaving, and rejoining the unemployed segment of society many times during their lives.

The modern father's problems in fulfilling the provider role have been complicated by a trend toward mothers assuming part of that role. More than half of the mothers in America with children under 18 years of age now hold jobs outside the home.

Children growing up in today's homes thus see fathers to whom providing is a constant struggle, a role that must be shared with the mother, a role in which the father often fails or sees himself as inadequate.

God the Father experiences no such frustrations. He created the universe, and he owns and controls it. To his resources there is no limit. "The silver is mine, and the gold is mine, saith the Lord of hosts" (Haggai 2:8). "For every beast of the forest is mine, and the cattle upon a thousand hills. I know all the fowls of the mountains: and the wild beasts of the field are mine" (Psalm 50:10, 11).

One of the most thrilling and liberating joys of being a Christian comes with acknowledging God the Father in the perfect fulfillment of his role as provider.

A friend of mine, one of the world's greatest Bible teachers, helped me to have a full understanding of what it means to be a child of God and have the Heavenly Father as your provider. The Holy Spirit used him to show me what a blessing it is to realize that God wants his children to trust him for every material need of life. I have recognized that in this world I don't own anything, that it all belongs to God.

When a washing machine breaks down, I say, "Lord, what are you going to do about your washer? It's broken." When someone runs a stop sign and crumples the car I'm making payments on, I say, "Lord, look what they've done to your car—and it's not even paid for."

It takes a crushing load off the shoulders of an earthly father to be able to tell a son or daughter, "I'm not your provider; God is your provider, and while he may sometimes use me and provide through me, it's really God who provides for all of us."

There is no contentment quite like that of knowing that you have God as your Father and that he is providing for you. And he never fails.

"My God shall supply all your need according to his riches in glory by Christ Jesus" (Philippians 4:19). "The earth is the Lord's, and the fullness thereof; the world, and they that dwell therein" (Psalm 24:1). "No good thing will he withhold from them that walk uprightly" (Psalm 84:11).

PART TWO

GOD AND CHILD DEVELOPMENT

5

FATHERHOOD:
A CHANNEL OF LOVE

The father is the child's primary link to the wider world outside the home. He introduces the child to the values, morals, and sex roles that our social system embraces. He exposes the child to the expectations of the world and encourages him to acquire the skills he will need and the responsibilities that will be imposed upon him.

The father accomplishes much of this contribution to his child's development unconsciously. As he takes the child to sports events, visits the zoo with him, or lets him tag along to the hardware store to pick up a wrench or a can of paint, the father may little realize that he is teaching the youngster anything. But actually such routine activities expose the child to the wide range of experiences needed to learn to develop personal relationships with other people to get along in the world. The mere presence of the father teaches the child invaluable lessons about life.

In modern society, however, fathers encounter almost as many difficulties in the socialization role as in their role as provider.

Separated from the children much of the day—in the case of the father who travels, much of the week— fathers can no longer be the source of occupational knowledge to their children that fathers once were. Occupational training is now left up to the schools.

Society sends conflicting messages to fathers concerning what values and morals they should teach their children. It also sends garbled and frequently changing advice as to what techniques the father should use to train and discipline children. The affluence, mobility, and freedom of the young also add to the modern American father's child-rearing problems. In fact, mobility has shattered the extended family in America, so that in few instances are grandparents, uncles, aunts, and cousins available for help. Also, a consensus on values cannot be found in most communities. Thus neighbors are no longer a reliable source of support for the father in child development.

God admirably fulfills the father's role in the socialization of children through the Holy Spirit, his written Word, and human instruments in the church.

The Holy Spirit gives the child of God a constant chaperone, a supervisory companion who never ceases to teach, train, and guide him. Christianity is described as a "walk," a word that aptly depicts the chain of experiences through which the Christian grows, not only as a child but on through adulthood. The Word of God, illuminated by the Holy Spirit, provides the child of God with a convenient, unchanging manual on the social skills that enable him to work and play successfully with others. The church acts as an extended family, giving the child the moral and spiritual support of an unlimited number of other people who love him and share his beliefs and aspirations.

On December 11, 1978, Robert Piest, a 15-year-old from Des Plaines, Illinois, disappeared. Since he had last been seen talking to a man named John Wayne Gacy, Jr. about a summer job, the police made a routine check of their files and discovered that Gacy had been convicted in Iowa in 1968 on a sodomy charge, but was paroled in 1970. The next day investigators found evidence at Gacy's home that led to his arrest—a class ring that had belonged to another missing boy.

In the days that followed, Gacy admitted that he had lured many boys and young men to his house for perverted sex, then murdered thirty-two of them. Following a map Gacy had drawn, police eventually found twenty-seven bodies under the house, where he had buried them and covered them with lime to suppress the odor and hasten decomposition. Gacy told police he threw the other five bodies in a river.

Gacy's story is important for more than the fact that it illustrates how wrong a person can go when socialization fails. It also illustrates that there are two kinds of socialization, a false kind and a true kind.

People who knew Gacy found it hard to believe he could have done such a thing. He was hard-working and popular in his community. He served on the Norwood Park Township Lighting Commission. The township committeeman who nominated him said he urged Gacy to take the job "based on his activity in the neighborhood." He said Gacy seemed to want to make it a "better place to live."

Gacy had indicated he wanted to run for public office. He had set out to be well-known, seizing opportunities to help people out. As part of this effort, he made a clown outfit and had himself photographed in it. He wore the clown suit to parties and entertained children with it in hospital wards.

On the surface, John Wayne Gacy, Jr. was an outstanding citizen, a properly socialized person who knew what the world expected of him. He seemed to know how to relate to other people.

But that was only a phony socialization disguising the deception and exploitation of others. John Wayne

Gacy, Jr. had not developed properly as a child. He had not internalized right values so that they became part of his character. He had merely used social skills to get what he wanted.

In many cases of sexual violence and murder, psychiatrists have been able to ferret out the nature of the developmental problems that produced the criminal personality. The trail almost always has led to failures of the socialization process very early in childhood.

This was the case with Juan Corona, convicted of killing and burying twenty-five farm workers in California in 1971; of Charles Whitman, who killed sixteen people and wounded thirty-two in a sniping attack from a University of Texas tower; of Howard Unruh, the World War II veteran who killed thirteen people at Camden, New Jersey, in 1949; and of Richard Speck, who killed eight nurses in their Chicago apartment in 1966. And according to some psychiatrists at this writing, it was the case with John Wayne Gacy, Jr.

In some of the above instances, the problem was found in the boy's relationship with his mother as a baby.

In the case of John Wayne Gacy, Jr.? An aunt in Chicago reported that Gacy had a "wonderful mother." But, she said, "he might have had a few problems with his father."

"A few problems with his father" can be enough to cause a boy to grow up with distorted conceptions of what the world and life are all about. "A few problems with his father," while it usually doesn't inflict such extensive damage to the personality, can lead to serious evil.

NURTURING

Psychiatrists often trace the roots of unacceptable behavior, including sex crime and mass murder, to "very early deprivation in nurturing."

Nurturance is a term social scientists use to describe a host of physical and nonphysical actions and attitudes by which parents demonstrate love and regard for a child. Nurturance fosters many of the qualities that enable a child to develop properly and to make a positive contribution to society as an adult. Such qualities include independence (in the sense of being able to make wise decisions on one's own), achievement, and a proper and secure sex orientation. Nurturing involves the giving of gifts, but this is not to be confused with provision of the child's needs as such. Giving as an act of nurture not only meets a physical need, but also communicates the parents' love and genuine personal interest in the child.

Nurturance is one of the key ingredients in the socialization of the child. Without it, a child may seem to assimilate the values taught by the parents without actually adopting them. Proper nurturance prepares the child mentally and emotionally to accept moral tenets and correct patterns for relationships with other people.

In the past, social scientists have thought of "nurturer" as a synonym for "woman." They've thought of the father as the breadwinner, a usually absent parent who contributed little to the nurturance of his children. Recently, though, they've discovered that fathers play an important role in nurturance.

Masculine nurturance may leave stronger and more lasting impressions than feminine nurturance because of the greater strength exhibited by the masculine parent when he hugs and cuddles his child. This impression of strength is believed to convey to the child an ability on the part of the father to protect and comfort him.

Fathers also are found to be more likely to pick up their children and handle them physically when they play with them. This is often more stimulating than mothers' play. For that reason, many children prefer to play with their fathers than their mothers.

All of these characteristics of father nurturance give a child the foundation he needs for proper socialization, especially when combined with genuine love. Michael Lamb wrote in *The Role of the Father in Child Development*: "It is extraordinarily important to remember that one of the most influential characteristics of the father-child relationship appears to be its warm and affectionate nature."

Unfortunately, many men fail to provide the father nurturance their children so desperately need. In *Father Power* Henry Biller and Dennis Meredith explain one of the reasons why: "Men in America, especially lower-class men, may be brought up almost entirely by women. Since the only people they see dealing with children are females, they get the idea that it is a definitely non-masculine responsibility. Wanting to be thoroughly male, they then avoid child care. . . . They deeply fear that caring for children will cause a loss of masculinity." There's simply no telling how much of the evil we see in today's world is traceable directly to this stupid, macho idea of masculinity.

Fathers make many other damaging mistakes in the area of nurturance simply because of ignorance. Usually such ignorance involves selfishness and a tendency to act from the wrong motives.

In giving, for instance, fathers often give the wrong things to their children for the wrong reasons. Some fathers, feeling guilty because of the little time they spend with their children, substitute gifts for involvement in the lives of their offspring. They seem to think that handing their child a doll or a football can take the place of a night at a father-daughter banquet or showing a son how to cast for bass on the shore of a lake. But substitutes don't work. They are the Brand X of nurturing. They always fall short.

Other fathers, prompted by their own feelings of insecurity, may use gifts to gain a sense of control over their children, to buy obedience. Still others may give to satisfy some obscure but demanding need of their own, not having the well-being of the child in mind at all.

While earthly fathers fail often, sometimes miserably, the Heavenly Father nurtures inerrantly. His love is everlasting, and he never ceases to express it in unmistakable ways. His motivations are always pure. The objective of his every action toward his children is to help them grow, to enable them to develop properly.

You may be wondering. "How does God nurture me? When has God ever picked me up?"

God the Father picked you up, if you're a Christian, at the moment you received Jesus Christ as your Lord and Savior. Jesus said, "My sheep hear my voice, and I know them, and they follow me: And I give unto them eternal life; and they shall never perish, neither shall any man pluck them out of my hand. My Father, which gave them me, is greater than all; and no man is able to pluck them out of my Father's hand" (John 10:27-29).

Talk about security! Talk about conveying an

impression of strength! How is that for nurturance?

An earthly father, assuming he was a good father, would hug you and play with you for a short while, then set you down and go on to some other interest. Your Heavenly Father will never put you down. Not only that, but he'll never let anyone or any power snatch you away from him. He is greater than all. He is stronger than any other power. You couldn't ask for any more effective nurturance than what our Heavenly Father provides.

Some earthly fathers, if they have the ability to do so, become overly protective of their children. They cuddle them so closely that the youngsters suffer from a lack of challenges and opportunities to grow and develop. They never get to try their wings.

God the Father, though greater than all, uses his power sparingly and wisely in the protection of his children. He allows them to encounter experiences that help them grow. The Bible says that Jesus himself learned "by the things which he suffered" (Hebrews 5:8). James counseled Christians to be glad when trials come, because trials develop patience and maturity (James 1:2-4). The trials God allows can be quite severe. But he promises that every experience he permits his children to be subjected to will be made to work for their benefit (Romans 8:28).

In the midst of trials and challenges that may be frightening, bewildering, and even painful, God provides priceless nurture in the form of comfort and peace of mind.

"Blessed be God, even the Father of our Lord Jesus Christ, the Father of mercies, and the God of all comfort; who comforteth us in all our tribulation, that we may be able to comfort them which are in any trouble, by the comfort wherewith we ourselves are comforted of God" (2 Corinthians 1:3, 4).

"And the peace of God, which passeth all understanding, shall keep [post a military guard around] your hearts and minds through Christ Jesus" (Philippians 4:7).

In the matter of nurturance, the Heavenly Father meets the needs of his children far beyond the ability of any earthly father to do so.

6

RAISING CONFIDENT CHILDREN

To be properly prepared for the challenges and opportunities of life, children need to develop confidence. "Confidence" is the term sociologists use to identify the complex system of attitudes and feelings that enable an individual to take a positive approach to life. Perhaps a better term would be "assurance" or, from the Christian perspective, "faith."

Earthly fathers bear a tremendous burden of responsibility in this aspect of their children's development. Since the father is such a big, strong authority figure in the home, the child tends to accept his word or attitude on nearly any subject as unquestionable truth.

Fathers must be careful to instill self-confidence by complimenting their children on their strengths. At the same time, they must be realistic in their appraisal of their children's abilities. It can be just as harmful to lead a child to expect too much of himself as too little. Fathers must help their children to evaluate their strengths, weaknesses, and limitations realistically.

The most common errors made by fathers in the confidence-building process are:

Being hypercritical.
Some fathers are never satisfied with their child's accomplishments. The child never hears a compliment or a word of encouragement, because the father invariably finds some slight fault in the performance or takes the attitude that "you could have done better."

Refusing to admit their own weaknesses.
The "superfather" can be a most discouraging influence on a child's life. Such a father never admits being wrong, never concedes that he has his own failures and shortcomings.

Belittling themselves before their children.
The opposite of the "superfather" is the one who habitually displays lack of confidence in himself. If a father is constantly running himself down in the presence of his children, he is presenting an image of insecurity the children are likely to copy.

Unlike the imperfect earthly father, God the Father recognizes and rewards every worthwhile accomplishment of his children. James 1:12 says, "Blessed is the man that endureth temptation: for when he is tried, he shall receive the crown of life, which the Lord hath promised to them that love him." Those who have stood strong in the Lord through times of trial know what a blessing it is to receive the approval of the Heavenly Father. Wearers of the "crown of life" feel twelve feet tall, because the power of God has made them "more than conquerors" (Romans 8:37).

The Heavenly Father never allows his children to overestimate their strengths, however. In 1 John 1:8 he reminds them that they all have weaknesses, they all have sinned. And in Romans 12:3 he warns them not to "think . . . more highly" of themselves than they should.

God is not a hypercritical father. He lets his children know how they can please him, and he applauds them when they do.

In Philippians 4:18, he reveals that it is "wellpleasing" to him when his children give to meet the need of another (in this case, the Apostle Paul). In Colossians 3:20, the Heavenly Father says it's "wellpleasing" to him for children to obey their earthly parents. In 1 Thessalonians 2:4, we find that the Heavenly Father is pleased when his children proclaim the true gospel. In Hebrews 13:21 we read it is "wellpleasing" to the Heavenly Father for his children to let his will be done in their lives.

In 1 John 3:22, God the Father tells us that he rewards his children—"whatsoever we ask, we receive of him"—when they "do those things that are pleasing in his sight."

Of course, God never belittles himself or admits weakness, because he has no weakness. He reveals himself just as he is, the creator and sustainer of the universe: "I am that I am" (Exodus 3:14). But there is no hypocrisy in God's presenting himself as perfect, as there is when imperfect earthly fathers do so. In fact, the knowledge that he is a child of a truly flawless Father is a tremendous source of confidence to the Christian.

While the Heavenly Father reveals himself as an all-powerful God, his children know he never uses that awesome power to harm or belittle them, for he also reveals himself as a loving Father. "Bless the Lord, O my soul, and forget not all his benefits: who forgiveth all thine iniquities; who healeth all thy diseases; who redeemeth thy life from destruction; who crowneth thee with lovingkindness and tender mercies; who satisfieth thy mouth with good things; so that thy youth is renewed like the eagle's" (Psalm 103:2-5).

To develop confidence, children need to know not only their fathers, but themselves, and the wise earthly father helps the child get to know himself. He helps him to understand not only how he should behave, but why he behaves as he does.

With their own limited understanding, earthly fathers work under a severe handicap in this regard. God's Word tells us, however, that the Heavenly Father knows his children: "O Lord, thou hast searched me, and known me. Thou knowest my downsitting and mine uprising; thou understandest my thought afar off. Thou compassest my path and my lying down, and art acquainted with all my ways. For there is not a word in my tongue, but, lo, O Lord, thou knowest it altogether.... Such knowledge is too wonderful for me; it is high, I cannot attain unto it" (Psalm 139:1-4, 6).

Yet 1 Corinthians tells us that the Heavenly Father shares this wonderful knowledge with his children: "But as it is written, Eye hath not seen, nor ear heard, neither have entered into the heart of man, the things which God hath prepared for them that love him. But God hath revealed them unto us by his Spirit: for the Spirit searcheth all things, yea, the deep things of God. . . . Now we have received, not the spirit of the world, but the spirit which is of God; that we might know the things that are freely given to us of God" (2:9, 10, 12).

In the seventh chapter of Romans, a passage too long to be reprinted here, the Heavenly Father reveals why his children behave as they do, sometimes doing things they know are wrong. God the Father works constantly to assure that his children possess a true knowledge of both their Father and themselves.

For fathers to instill confidence in their children, it is imperative that they show sincere interest in their children's lives and become involved in their activities. As I've already pointed out, the conditions of an industrialized society limit the earthly father's ability to fulfill this part of his role.

Psalm 139:17, 18 describes the Heavenly Father's interest in his children as more constant and more intense than any earthly father's could ever be: "How precious also are thy thoughts unto me, O God! How great is the sum of them! If I should count them, they are more in number than the sand: when I awake I am still with thee."

It would be impossible for a father to be more involved in the life of a child than the Heavenly Father is in the lives of his children. Jesus said in his prayer to the Father: "And the glory which thou gavest me I have given them; that they may be one, even as we are one: I in them, and thou in me, that they may be made perfect [complete] in one. . . ."

How could the Heavenly Father be more involved with you than to be one with you?

INDEPENDENCE

"Independence," like "confidence," is a term from the lexicon of the social scientist. To the humanist, "independence" may mean freedom from accountability to God or freedom from the moral values of parents or society. Christians realize that it's neither possible nor desirable to be independent from their Heavenly Father or his codes of behavior. In fact, the very basis for spiritual maturity is in the Christian's recognizing and accepting his state of total dependence upon God.

Independence has another meaning, however, that is completely in accord with Christian precepts. In this context, independence is not freedom from authority, but the freedom that comes with a decision made in response to the counsel of God; i.e., subjection to proper authority. It is not the freedom to do whatever one wants to do, but the freedom to refuse to do what the world wants one to do if it conflicts with the will of God.

The Apostle Paul spoke of this sort of independence in Romans 12:1, 2—"I beseech you therefore, brethren, by the mercies of God, that ye present your bodies a living sacrifice, holy, acceptable unto God, which is your reasonable service. And be not conformed to this world: but be ye transformed by the renewing of your mind, that ye may prove [demonstrate] what is that good, and acceptable, and perfect, will of God."

Earthly fathers make many mistakes in developing independence in their children. They push them into experiences and decisions before they are ready, or they shelter them too much and prevent them from developing skill in decision-making, or they teach them to seek the wrong kind of independence, the kind that shows no respect for authority and leads to a life of bitterness and rebellion.

The Heavenly Father presents a beautiful formula for independence, an independence that demonstrates to the world that good and perfect will of God. We are to present our "bodies a living sacrifice . . . unto God."

Those who do so will be transformed by the renewing of their mind. They will be independent in that they won't be "conformed to this world." They won't be compelled to do something just because "everybody's doing it." They'll be independent from the temptations and pressures of the world.

To be independent from the world is to know God the Father in the truest and most intimate sense. ". . . I will dwell in them, and walk in them; and I will be their God, and they shall be my people. Wherefore come out from among them, and be ye separate, saith the Lord, and touch not the unclean thing; and I will receive you, and will be a Father unto you, and ye shall be my sons and daughters, saith the Lord Almighty" (2 Corinthians 6:16-18).

God's Word paints an even more dramatic picture of the meaning of independence for his children in Psalm 18. Verses 2, 4 and 17 read: "The Lord is my rock, and my fortress, and my deliverer; my God, my strength, in whom I will trust; my buckler, and the horn of my salvation, and my high tower. . . . The sorrows of death compassed me, and the floods of ungodly men made me afraid. . . . He delivered me from my strong enemy, and from them which hated me: for they were too strong for me."

As he experiences the infinite love, strength, and mercy of his Heavenly Father, the child of God develops a confidence surpassing any that an earthly father could impart to him.

ACHIEVEMENT MOTIVATION

In the world, the prize goes to those who have "get up and go." The highly motivated ones, those who have an innate desire to "get ahead," usually are the ones willing to pay the price in sweat and discipline to ascend the ladder of "success," however they might define that term.

Sociologists say the father's expectations are most important in developing motivation to achieve in his children. If the father expects little of his child, the child will achieve little. If the father himself is a low achiever, he is likely to be critical, rejecting, and contemptuous of his children. These attitudes rob children of motivation. They never achieve simply because they don't want to achieve. They don't see or appreciate the rewards for accomplishment.

Some elements of society hinder fathers in instilling motivation in their children. In America a large and vocal counterculture movement encourages "dropping out" and belittles achievement.

To do an effective job of instilling motivation, fathers must somehow help their children develop a certain assertiveness. For Christians, this doesn't mean a cocky or intimidating air. It means simply an ability to be firm, forthright, and determined in setting goals and attaining them.

Closely associated with achievement motivation is career choice. Fathers have a definite and very important role in this too.

Many earthly fathers completely botch their responsibilities in these areas. Not only do they often employ the wrong tactics to create motivation, but they misguide their children as to the meaning of success and point them toward the wrong goals.

Certainly the Heavenly Father does not expect too little of his children. He expects no less than perfection or complete spiritual maturity. Ephesians 4:12, 13 says, "For the perfecting [equipping] of the saints, for the work of the ministry, for the edifying of the body of Christ: Till we all come in the unity of the faith, and of the knowledge of the Son of God, unto a perfect [mature] man, unto the measure of the stature of the fullness of Christ."

God the Father promises that success will come no matter how rugged the path. "And let us not be weary in well doing: for in due season we shall reap, if we faint not" (Galatians 6:9).

The Heavenly Father instills in his children the

greatest motivational force in the universe—love. The Apostle Paul describes that irresistible motivation in these terms: "For the love of Christ constraineth us; because we thus judge, that if one died for all, then were all dead: And that he died for all, that they which live should not henceforth live unto themselves, but unto him which died for them, and rose again" (2 Corinthians 5:14, 15).

What more simple, more reasonable, more powerful motivation could there be? His love moved him to die for us. Love should move us to live for him.

That's the general goal that God the Father points his children toward—loving him and living for him. But God also has a specific will, or I should say many specific wills, for his children. Many of his children fret in searching for this, but I believe finding God's will is usually a simple matter for anyone who is genuinely committed to doing it.

The first step in discovering God's specific will is for the child of God to come to the place where he can truthfully say, as Jesus said in the Garden of Gethsemane, "Not my will, but thine be done."

At the risk of oversimplifying something that has troubled many Christians for months and even years, I believe that the moment you can say "Thy will be done" and really mean it, God's will for your life becomes simply whatever it is you want to do and have the ability to do. Listen to his own Word on the matter: "Trust in the Lord, and do good; so shalt thou dwell in the land, and verily thou shalt be fed. *Delight thyself also in the Lord; and he shall give thee the desires of thine heart.* Commit thy way unto the Lord; trust also in him; and he shall bring it to pass" (Psalm 34:3, 4).

Many of God's children seem to have the mistaken

idea that to do God's will they must give up what they enjoy doing. That may be true in some cases, but I doubt that it's true when the child is genuinely committed to pleasing the Father. I believe that for children who "delight in the Lord," God's will is to give them the desires of their hearts.

At any rate, we know that God wants his children to succeed in the best possible sense of the word. Everything he does and says toward his children is to motivate them and encourage them to be productive citizens in his kingdom.

Sometimes it seems to the child of God that the Heavenly Father's methods in pursuing this goal are a bit harsh. Jesus compared it to the pruning of a vine: "I am the true vine, and my Father is the husbandman. Every branch in me that beareth not fruit he taketh away: and every branch that beareth fruit, he purgeth it, that it may bring forth more fruit" (John 15:1, 2).

When God's pruning becomes painful, his children need only remember that the "husbandman's" purpose is not to injure the vine, but to bring it to its full potential.

The child of the Heavenly Father never suffers for lack of motivation to achieve. And he is motivated to achieve that which is worthwhile, that which pleases God.

7

TO DISCIPLINE WITH LOVE

Probably in no area of the child development process is there more confusion among American parents than in the area of discipline. Countless volumes have been written by self-proclaimed "experts" on the subject. Many of these are sociologists or psychologists whose credentials are weak with respect to actual experience in successful child-rearing.

For many years, the trend in parental education has been to warn against corporal punishment. Instead of physical discipline, the experts prescribe warm parent-child relationships and permissiveness. Such ideas run counter to the "natural" tendency of parents to discipline their children physically.

Fathers as a whole lean more toward physical discipline than mothers. Perhaps for that reason, perhaps not, fathers often emerge as the primary authority figure in the household. When a discipline problem arises, mothers are prone to call in the father for support. Fathers who administer physical discipline with love and restraint usually are quite successful in rearing their children to be well-adjusted, achievement-oriented young people and adults.

Perhaps because of the widespread abuse of physical punishment, however, expert advice on the subject continues to weigh heavily against the use of such methods. To many fathers, this quasi-official disapproval of their natural tendencies results in discouragement and guilt feelings. Other factors add further frustrations.

This being an industrialized, urban society, most children have large blocks of leisure time and enormous amounts of unused energy. As a result, young people are very active. And with motorized transportation readily available, their activites are likely to take place far from the supervisory eyes of their earthly fathers. Also, contemporary counsel says to be permissive toward children, to let them develop their interests and "find themselves."

All of these factors combine to cause many fathers to feel they have no control over their children. And in many cases the facts give more than a trace of support for such a feeling. As a result, fathers often experience feelings of guilt and depression and eventually of despair from what they regard as failure in their role in the discipline of their children.

Earthly fathers often are surprised and relieved to learn that the Heavenly Father's advice on physical discipline conflicts with that of most secular "experts" on the subject. God warns against physical or psychological abuse of children: "And, ye fathers, provoke not your children to wrath. . ." (Ephesians 6:4). But he prescribes physical correction, as in Proverbs 13:24: "He that spareth his rod hateth his son: but he that loveth him chasteneth him betimes."

Discipline involves much more than physical punishment, of course. It entails the issuing of clear rules and instructions, fairness in enforcing those rules, forgiveness, and gentleness. It also involves types of punishment other than physical punishment.

One example is the withdrawal of privileges. Children should be taught from earliest childhood that when rules are broken, privileges will be withdrawn. The withdrawal should not be permanent, however, since this may cause resentment and so defeat the purpose of the discipline.

Expressions of disapproval can be used effectively as a disciplinary measure. The father must be careful, however. He must make perfectly clear that his disapproval is directed toward the undesirable behavior and not toward the child himself.

Incentives can be used in connection with achievement, but never as rewards for proper or moral behavior. For example, a child can be promised a special treat for performing some chore above and beyond the duties normally required of members of the family, but he or she should never be rewarded materially for obedience to the moral laws of God, society, and the family. Every child needs to learn that he or she is expected to perform certain standard duties and obey moral and ethical rules without reward.

The key to the successful use of these various methods is wisdom. Using physical punishment when another disciplinary method would be more instructive can be a tragic mistake. Avoiding physical punishment in favor of other methods, when physical punishment is called for, can be an even greater error.

Any parent who has tried to rear children realizes that the wisdom to do and say the right thing at the right time is not part of the equipment of the natural father, acting on his own. Fathers and mothers are simply not smart enough, in their own wisdom, to discipline children properly. God the Father, and he alone, possesses the wisdom needed for the discipline task. While the Bible is not a manual on child discipline, it does give more specific instructions than many people believe. Yet the most important secrets to successful child-rearing are found more in the spirit than in the letter. To those who know God as Father, the Holy Spirit is a constant companion, guiding them into all truth (John 16:13), the truth about child discipline as well as other things.

Even with the Bible and the Holy Spirit, however, the earthly father will never be perfect. Everyone needs a Heavenly Father. And certainly the Heavenly Father knows how to discipline his children properly. ". . . My son, despise not thou the chastening of the Lord, nor faint when thou art rebuked of him: for whom the Lord loveth he chasteneth, and scourgeth every son whom he receiveth. If ye endure chastening, God dealeth with you as with sons; for what son is he whom the father chasteneth not?" (Hebrews 12:5-7).

God the Father is a loving Father who disciplines with wisdom.

8
CHILDREN AND SEX ROLES

By giving homosexuals the boldness to "come out of the closet," the "gay liberation" movement has revealed the extent and seriousness of improper sex orientation in the United States. Gay militants assert that one in every ten Americans is attracted sexually by members of the same sex. Militants invariably play a numbers game in seeking to win public acceptance of their cause and it may be that gays have exaggerated the number of homosexuals for political purposes. Still, there's no denying that homosexuality is a widespread problem in our country today.

While some homosexuals try to blame their condition on genetic factors, many social researchers insist that homosexuality is a result of environment, not heredity. In short, they attribute it to a breakdown in the child's socialization process. Something goes wrong in the child's psychological development very early in life, causing the child to acquire an improper sexual orientation that is extremely difficult to change later on.

Recent studies suggest that sex-typing is established much earlier than had previously been supposed. By the time a child is eighteen months old, it's now believed, he or she has largely completed the process of sex-role adoption. From this point, it becomes steadily more difficult to correct any error in the process.

What actually goes on in the process of sex-typing or sex-role adoption? While the answer to that question remains largely a mystery, social scientists have learned a few things about it.

To the social scientist, the terms male and female refer to the biological makeup of the child. Children are born, except in very rare cases, with distinctly male or female biological characteristics. The terms masculine and feminine, on the other hand, are viewed as psychological in nature. They are characteristics acquired by the child in the psychological development process.

The ideal in child development, of course, is for the child born biologically male to become psychologically masculine and for the child born biologically female to become psychologically feminine. As one social scientist puts it, "Possessing a secure masculinity or femininity means being happily male or female."

Establishing proper sex-role orientation is basic to personality development. When the sex-typing process fails, the damage affects more than just the sex life of the child and the adult he or she will become. It affects the entire personality.

The father, social scientists say, is usually more concerned about sex roles than the mother. One explanation for this is that the father, for reasons not yet clearly understood, is more involved than the mother in the type of learning that occurs without explicit instruction or enforcement, "observational learning." Observational learning, by which the child learns merely by observing the parent model, is seen as the crucial process in the sex-role development of young children.

The father's role in the development of a son's masculinity is of obvious importance. Simply stated, the process consists of the son's getting to know what a man is like by watching the behavior, attitudes, and mannerisms displayed by his father. Boys deprived of an adequate male model may develop abnormal sex-role orientation. The lack of a male model thrusts a son into a continuous search for a father figure, and he sometimes seeks to satisfy his need through a homosexual relationship.

As I noted earlier, the search can also lead to blind subservience to false "fathers" like Rev. Jim Jones or Charles Manson, or to gnawing frustrations that find release in irrational violence, as in the case of snipers Charles Whitman and Howard Unruh.

While the father's influence in the son's development has long been recognized, his role in the development of the daughter is just beginning to be understood. Girls may learn as much or more through the role modeling of the father as do boys. A close relationship with her father enables a daughter to have not only a close romantic relationship with another man—her husband—later in life, but also other kinds of close relationships with people of both sexes.

How does a father exert such a powerful influence in the sex-typing process of his daughter? For the most part, he does it unconsciously, simply by living and behaving like a man.

Fathers who have developed masculine personalities like their daughters to behave like "little ladies." Therefore, they tend to reward and encourage dependent, dainty, feminine behavior and discourage rough, coarse, masculine behavior. In so doing, they facilitate their daughters' feminine sex-role adoption. They are the judges of femininity whose unspoken pronouncements keep their daughters posted on "how they are doing" in developing feminine or womanly traits.

Social studies find that women with unstable sex lives and broken marriages are more likely to report poor relationships with their fathers than with their mothers. Girls from father-absent homes show a greater tendency to be seductive than girls from two-parent homes.

Father-deficiency also contributes more than mother-deficiency to the development of female homosexuality, social scientists believe. Female homosexuals, or lesbians, fall into two categories, "masculine" and "feminine." The masculine lesbian is likely to see her father as weak or incompetent. Her homosexuality results from her unconscious effort to fulfill within herself the need for a male model that her father failed to provide. The feminine lesbian is likely to describe her father as puritanical, exploitative, or fear-inducing in his behavior toward her. As a result, she rejects natural sexual relationships as either sinful and dirty, or merely frightening. Her rejection of natural sex makes her prey to the recruitment and training of the aggressive masculine lesbian.

In the case of both sons and daughters, the key to a successful father relationship seems to be love and warmth, though these alone are not enough. A father also must be an assertive, involved model of masculinity to his children. But machismo without warmth can be as damaging as any other deficiency in the father's role modeling. Case histories of many homosexuals point to the psychologically distorting influence of either a hostile or cool, indifferent father as a major cause.

The relationship between the father and the mother

is also of prime importance. Living in a family where there is a close, warm marital relationship helps a child immeasurably to gain a sense of security and develop a positive model of male-female affection.

In his role as Father, God provides both sons and daughters with the perfect sex-role model. As he reveals himself through his written Word, he unfolds the characteristics of a true father. He shows himself to be warm, loving, protective, concerned. He involves himself directly in the interests and activities of his children. He reveals himself to be a person of strength mingled with tenderness, of judgment tempered by mercy. To him, no normal function of the body, including physical sex, is sinful, wrong, or dirty in itself. He ordains certain ways for the biological and psychological needs of his children to be fulfilled, and he warns that trying to fulfill these needs in any other way leads to destruction. Yet he does not condemn us for being aware of the needs and wanting them fulfilled. He created us with these needs and his desire for us is that they should be fulfilled to the utmost. His instructions are meant to keep us from being cheated of this fulfillment by following the counterfeit plans offered by Satan and the world.

The God-ordained way for our sexual needs to be fulfilled is through marriage—marriage that endures until "death do us part." The two shall become "one flesh," God said. Only in oneness do the male and female realize the fulfillment of their sexual needs.

Every other plan of sexual fulfillment is a Satanic counterfeit. Premarital sex, which the Bible calls fornication, and extramarital sex, which the Bible calls adultery, are counterfeits. All of the varieties of homosexuality, which the Bible also condemns, are counterfeits as well. None of these deviations from

God's plan offer fulfillment. Those who pursue them lead lives marked by frustration, disillusionment, desperation, and misery. Even many of the social scientists who once viewed these plans as "acceptable alternatives" to conventional sex now admit that a growing mound of evidence indicates these alternatives never lead to genuine satisfaction, that they invariably lead to emptiness and in many cases to disintegration of the personality.

The Heavenly Father never makes the mistakes that so many earthly fathers make. He doesn't equate manliness with roughness, crudeness, or violence. He doesn't confuse effeminacy with gentleness. He encourages sons to develop masculinity and daughters femininity in the true sense of those terms. He doesn't point his sons in the direction of lust and lechery, and he doesn't teach his daughters to think or behave as sex objects for the pleasure of men.

God the Father teaches his sons and daughters to be individuals with great dignity. He trains them to regard others in the same light and to relate to them as brothers and sisters in the household of God.

You won't find many passages in the Bible where God inspired one of his writers to say, "Now this is what it means to be a man," or "This is what it means to be a woman." However, his instructions regarding these matters are woven into the fabric of the Scriptures. They are found in the role models God gives in the form of those whom he has chosen to represent him through the ages. He chose the heroes and heroines of the faith not only to reveal himself, but also to reveal what men and women, boys and girls were to be like in the family of God.

Sociologists say the sex roles taught in the family are primarily the expectations imposed by society as a whole. In our society, and most others around the world, these expectations are generally drawn from the Word of God. Men and women through the ages have found biblical sex roles to be the proper roles, the roles that best serve both individuals and societies.

That's why attacks on "old-fashioned" roles and customs in our society are so dangerous. They are not attacks merely against traditions of men. They are assaults upon God's ordained methods and institutions. Such attacks threaten the foundations of society, because they tamper with the socialization process by which women become women, men become men, and orderly society is perpetuated.

When the family deteriorates, as is happening in America, and the father's role in child development suffers, all the ills of father-deficiency can be expected to proliferate. We can expect enormous upsurges in cultism, drug and alcohol addiction, criminality, and homosexuality unless America's father-deficiency is overcome. And it will be overcome only if America can be turned to the Heavenly Father. Earthly fathers can't completely fulfill their father role in the sex-typing of their children even when they are "good fathers" by the world's standards. No one is complete apart from God:

"Ye are complete in him, which is the head of all principality and power" (Colossians 2:10).

One of the world's best-known born-again Christians and Bible scholars has said, "It takes God to make a man." He could have said "a man or a woman."

9

HELPING CHILDREN GROW

How do children grow emotionally, intellectually, and spiritually, and what do fathers contribute to this?

EMOTIONAL DEVELOPMENT

Emotional development is more necessary for fulfillment in life than is physical development. Without sound emotional health, the most physically robust child can grow up to be a failure and disappointment.

The basis for proper emotional development is a favorable self-image. How a child learns to think of himself has everything to do with how he or she thinks about life and about other people. If a child grows up thinking of himself as inferior or unworthy, he almost certainly will have problems in his relations with others and in reaching his full potential.

Nurturance by the father is crucial to a child's development of a favorable self-image. The father's attitude toward the child's mental and emotional makeup helps establish the child's attitude toward himself.

What the social scientists call "body pride" determines to a great degree what a child thinks about himself. Body pride involves the child's basic feelings about his body—its soundness, its ability, and its appearance. Fathers can help their children to develop physically, of course, and good fathers certainly will do so. But they can help much more in the area of emotional development, the area involving feelings their children have about their own bodies. The father who belittles or pokes fun at his child's physical limitations or appearance can cripple the child emotionally for life. The father who speaks encouragingly to his child in regard to his or her physical prowess or appearance can produce, even in a child with a physical handicap, an emotional strength that will see the child through life's toughest challenges. Fathers can contribute substantially to their children's emotional development by instilling in them a sense of competence and a sense of security.

In the area of competence, fathers help most by showing their children how to use their abilities. Wise fathers start the process when their children are babes. They begin with the simplest challenges, then encourage them to try increasingly difficult tasks. Again, attitudes are more important than techniques. To build a sense of competence in a child, the father's attitude must always be such as to make the child feel gratified and fulfilled by what he can do and not crushed by what he can't do.

Fathers have a key role in creating a sense of security in their children primarily because the father is the bigger, stronger and more imposing parent. Nothing helps a child's sense of security more than to see this big, strong, imposing, competent person "on his side," protecting and loving him and helping him reach his potential.

Emotional problems confront every growing child. These emotional problems invariably have their roots in other areas, whether intellectual, physical, or moral. As these problems arise, fathers often are called upon for therapeutic services. They are asked to become counselors and problem-solvers. Most fathers have little training for this task, yet they have the duty and responsibility to perform it. Fathers motivated by love and concern for their children's well-being can do a creditable job.

The child's greatest need is usually what social scientists call "stroking." The Bible calls it comforting. In essence, this consists simply of words and actions that let the child know that there is someone who cares, that raise the child's status in his own eyes, that help him make correct decisions, that reward him for standing firm for right even if all his peers seem to be against him.

Even the best earthly fathers commit errors that hinder the emotional development of their children. In a stressful moment they may speak some word or display some attitude that the child reads as disapproval of him physically or mentally. The child's self-worth is injured, perhaps without the father's knowing it.

Earthly fathers spend an average of only twenty minutes a day with their children. In so short a span, they can hardly contribute as much as they should to their children's development of skills or engender a sense of competence. Being such an imposing authority figure, they are as likely to intimidate their children as they are to instill in them a sense of security.

In the area of counseling, the sad fact is that most earthly fathers are bumbling incompetents. Lacking the wisdom to give proper counsel, they try to cover up with bluster and scolding. Far from the "stroking" their children need, earthly fathers are likely to dish out discouragement. Rather than helping their children solve their problems, they are apt to rebuke and belittle them for having the problems.

The Heavenly Father is the perfect father when it comes to aiding emotional development.

Take the all-important factor of self-image, for example. What could be more wholesome for a child's self-concept than the knowlege that God made him the way he is and that God has the ability either to change him, if that's his will, or to use him effectively in spite of what the child may regard as "defects"?

God the Father leaves no room for doubt that he has made each of us, individually. "Thy hands have made me and fashioned me. . ." (Psalm 119:73). "My substance was not hid from thee, when I was made in secret, and curiously wrought in the lowest parts of the earth. Thine eyes did see my substance, yet being unperfect; and in thy book all my members were written, which in continuance were fashioned, when as yet there was none of them" (Psalm 139:15, 16).

Some of the most confident, radiant human beings I have ever seen have been people with withered hands or twisted legs. Despite physical disabilities severe enough to make a whole person weep with sympathy, these people live lives of joy and fulfillment because they know they are children of God and because they accept the fact that God has made them as they are and is using them in their crippled state.

The Heavenly Father knows how to instill in his children the feelings of competence and security that are so vital to their emotional well-being. The secret is summed up in the words of Paul in Philippians 4:13: "I can do all things through Christ which strengtheneth me." The child of God learns to depend on the strength and wisdom of his Father, rather than on his own prowess. He follows the example of Jesus, who said: "The Son can do nothing of himself, but what he seeth the Father do: for what things soever he doeth, these also doeth the Son likewise" (John 5:19).

"If ye love me, keep my commandments. And I will pray the Father, and he shall give you another Comforter, that he may abide with you for ever; Even the Spirit of truth. . . . I will not leave you comfortless: I will come to you. . . . If a man love me, he will keep my words: and my Father will love him, and we will come unto him, and make our abode with him. . . . But the Comforter, which is the Holy Spirit, whom the Father will send in my name, he shall teach you all things, and bring all things to your remembrance, whatsoever I have said unto you" (John 14:15-18, 23, 26).

These verses are not normally cited as "security" verses, but in regard to the Heavenly Father's relationship with his children, they may be the most important "security" verses in the Bible. They promise that the entire Trinity, not only the Father but the Son and the Holy Spirit, are intimately involved in the life of the child of God for all eternity.

Jesus promises that the Holy Spirit will be sent to abide with the child of God "for ever." He promises that he himself will come to the believer to make doubly sure that he is never alone. He adds that he will bring the Heavenly Father with him and that they both will "make our abode" with the child of God. Finally, Jesus promises that the Holy Spirit will constantly teach the child of God, instructing him in every step of life and reminding him continually of the specific will of the Father and the Lord Jesus Christ for his life.

No earthly father could begin to offer security like that. In the Heavenly Father, the child of God has the most competent and effective therapist the world has ever known. He is not only able but willing to help his children with any problem that confronts them. He pleads with them to cast all their cares upon him because he cares for them (1 Peter 5:7).

The Father's written Word holds true counsel for the real problems of life. His Word is more specific in dealing with our problems than most of us give it credit for being. It is not by chance that the prophet Isaiah identified the Messiah as "Wonderful, Counselor" (9:6). "Unless thy law had been my delights, I should then have perished in mine affliction. I will never forget thy precepts: for with them thou hast quickened me [brought me to life]" (Psalm 119:92, 93).

Through his wise counsel, the Heavenly Father administers the "stroking," the comfort or encouragement, that his child so desperately needs. "Remember the word unto thy servant, upon which thou hast caused me to hope. This is my comfort in my affliction: for thy word hath quickened me [given me life]" (Psalm 119:49, 50).

God the Father promises that he will never fail his children if they will only bring their problems to him. Most Christians learn early in their life in the family of God the familiar entreaty of Proverbs 3:5, 6— "Trust in the Lord with all thine heart; and lean not unto thine own understanding. In all thy ways acknowledge him, and he shall direct thy paths." No better formula for sound emotional development has ever been written.

INTELLECTUAL DEVELOPMENT

The father contributes much to the intellectual development of the child. Contact with the father can be an exciting mind-expanding adventure, creating inquisitiveness, the ability to analyze situations, and the ability to apply reason in problem-solving in children.

Fathers can also help the child to acquire verbal skill, to build a vocabulary. Each new experience spawns a new generation of "What's that, Daddy?" "What does it do?" "Why?" Answering these endless inquiries, while it may become an exasperating chore to even the most patient father, adds little by little to the child's expanding store of knowledge. It is said a child learns more in his first six years than in the remainder of his lifespan. At any rate, there can be little doubt that what he learns in these formative years forms the intellectual base on which his future knowledge and wisdom will rest.

Wise fathers make the most of these formative years by deliberately increasing the range of experiences the child is exposed to. Such fathers stay on the alert for opportunities to allow their children to view things from different perspectives. They supplement "real-life" experiences with well-chosen reading matter. They take them on individualized field trips to help them understand the answers to some of their questions. As their children enter school, they encourage them to study and learn. They reward them when they excel, and they challenge them to try harder when they need improvement. They eagerly accept opportunities to become involved in schoolwork with their children and attend school competitions and other education-oriented functions with them.

Few things offer a concerned father more challenge and more gratification than helping his child develop intellectually and seeing firsthand the exciting results of his effort. Many fathers realize and take advantage of this marvelous opportunity to contribute to the growth of another person's mind—their own son's or their own daughter's.

Unfortunately many earthly fathers never know or become involved in this delightful experience. As a result, many young people reach adulthood without having developed anywhere near their potential intellectually. Compared to what they could be, they are mental midgets. They are the educational dropouts and the functional illiterates that contribute little to society. They are the don't-care students who make learning difficult for those who do care. They are the undisciplined legions who are driving thousands of quality educators out of the schools and into other fields.

In God the Father, any growing young mind finds a Parent who is intensely and unwaveringly interested in his intellectual development. Many Scriptures associate knowledge or wisdom and a personal relationship with the Heavenly Father and Jesus Christ.

The entire book of Proverbs is dedicated to that very theme. It begins with this statement of its purpose: "To know wisdom and instruction; to perceive the words of understanding; to receive the instruction of wisdom, justice, and judgment, and equity; to give subtilty to the simple, to the young man knowledge and discretion" (1:2-4).

Verse 5 continues, "A wise man will hear, and will increase learning; and a man of understanding shall attain unto wise counsels." Verse 7 sets forth the basis for all wisdom: "The fear of the Lord is the beginning of knowledge."

The book continues with one plea after another for the children of God to heed the instructions of their Heavenly Father: "Hear, ye children, the instruction of a father, and attend to know understanding. For I give you good doctrine, forsake ye not my law" (4:1, 2).

"Get wisdom, get understanding: forget it not; neither decline from the words of my mouth. Forsake her not, and she shall preserve thee: love her, and she shall keep thee. Wisdom is the principal thing; therefore get wisdom: and with all thy getting get understanding" (4:5-7).

Perhaps the most important exhortation of all appears in verses 20-22: "My son, *attend to my words;* incline thine ear unto my sayings. Let them not depart from thine eyes; keep them in the midst of thine heart. *For they are life unto those that find them,* and health to all their flesh."

This is the message modern America has sadly overlooked. Not all knowledge and not all "wisdom" are of equal value. It's possible for a child to develop a brilliant intellect and still be a failure in life. The words of wisdom that God gives are "life unto those that find them." Much of the knowledge many earthly fathers impart to their youngsters is false or destructive knowledge, leading to death. The Heavenly Father assures his children that "I have taught thee in the way of wisdom; I have led thee in right paths" (4:11).

Much of the educational failure visible today in America can be attributed to the fact that God and his word have been omitted from the curriculum of so many American young people. The great failure in American education is not that so many of the nation's youth emerge from the schools unable to read and write on a functional level. Rather, it's the fact that so many even among the brightest of them are spiritually illiterate. They have never been introduced to the Heavenly Father, the eternal fountain of life-giving wisdom. The Word of God is not a textbook on language or science. But it *is* a textbook on life, and without a working knowledge of its contents there is no true language and no true science.

Too many modern intellectuals send young people on a sort of mystical odyssey in search of "truth." Jesus, in his prayer to the Heavenly Father in John 17, said, "Thy word is truth" (verse 17).

In the first verses of his Gospel, John referred to Jesus as "the Word." The word used in the original Greek was *Logos*, which meant ultimate wisdom, infinite knowledge. John also refers to Jesus as the Light. Jesus is the divine understanding that can illumine the minds of men and enable them to perceive genuine truth, unobscured reality. By his indwelling Holy Spirit, he promises to guide God's children "into all truth" (John 16:13).

The search for truth offered by humanistic education leads to a captivating journey through darkness. God the Father's truth offers a liberating walk in the light. Jesus said, in a passage often taken out of context and twisted by the humanists to serve their purposes, "And ye shall know the truth, and the truth shall make you free" (John 8:32).

Jesus did not mean that just any knowledge is truth, or that merely accumulating a vast store of facts would make you free. The line must be read along with the preceding verses before Jesus' meaning becomes clear. In context, Jesus' statement reads like this:

"Then said Jesus unto them, When ye have lifted up the Son of man, then shall ye know that I am he, and that I do nothing of myself; but as my Father hath taught me, I speak these things. And he that sent me is with me: the Father hath not left me alone; for I do always those things that please him. As he spoke these words, many believed on him. Then said Jesus to those Jews which believed on him, If ye continue in my word, then are ye my disciples indeed; and ye shall know the truth, and the truth shall make you free" (John 8:28-32).

This passage is the missing link in the education of the average American child. It reveals that the Heavenly Father lives with his children, teaching them at every step of their way. Life's every experience is a field trip. Jesus demonstrated this "walking classroom" by his own life. To enroll in this class, the passage teaches, the "pupil" has only to believe in Jesus, to accept him by faith as Lord and Savior. As those who do so continue to follow Jesus and to live in his word, they know the truth—the real truth from God—and *that* truth makes them free.

Apart from the enlightenment the Heavenly Father can provide, no child or adult can ever achieve full intellectual development.

MORAL DEVELOPMENT

In a book about God the Father, it seems almost superfluous to talk about moral development. The Heavenly Father is of course intensely interested in the moral development of his children. In the Ten Commandments, he has given them the greatest moral code ever written.

Even secular sociologists concede that all of the traits of personality development discussed thus far operate within a framework of morality. They describe morality as simply the process by which a child learns to make decisions about what is right and what is wrong, feels guilt when that feeling is appropriate and feels the necessity for confessing misdeeds.

Every child develops a sense of right and wrong. The values may be distorted; they may not coincide with those of society or of God, but they exist nevertheless. The question is not whether the child will develop moral values, but whether he will develop values that stand to benefit or to harm himself and others.

The father's role in the moral development of children is unique and vital. Fathers who rely on love-oriented discipline perform most effectively in this role. Literature on the subject indicates juvenile delinquents are far more likely to come from father-deficient homes than from stable two-parent homes. When fathers are frequently absent or when they are antisocial, unempathetic, and hostile, children are likely to have trouble in their moral development.

In what Jesus pinpointed as the two great commandments, God the Father laid the foundation for the supreme system of moral values. He said: "Thou shalt love the Lord thy God with all thy heart, and with all thy soul, and with all thy mind. This is the first and great commandment. And the second is like unto it, Thou shalt love thy neighbor as thyself" (Matthew 22:37-39).

If a child of God is totally committed to his Father and if he loves his neighbor as he loves himself, he would certainly live a life characterized by doing good toward both God and his fellowman.

Too many earthly fathers instill just the opposite kind of moral foundation in their children. They teach them to serve only themselves. As a result, their every moral decision is based on what they perceive to be best for themselves, not for God or others. But they cheat themselves. For as Jesus said, "Whosoever will save his life shall lose it: and whosoever will lose his life for my sake shall find it" (Matthew 16:25).

God the Father doesn't just hand his children a book of his moral laws; he also tells them how they can succeed in keeping them. "Neither yield ye your members as instruments of unrighteousness unto sin: but yield yourselves unto God, as those that are alive from the dead, and your members as instruments of righteousness unto God" (Romans 6:13).

Human nature yearns to do the things that bring misery and death, but the Heavenly Father gives instructions on how to overcome human nature and live a full abundant life. "For if ye live after the flesh, ye shall die: but if ye through the Spirit do mortify [put to death] the deeds of the body, ye shall live" (Romans 8:13).

Whereas earthly fathers often are far from their children when moral guidance is needed, the Heavenly Father (represented by the Holy Spirit) lives within his children day in and day out. He is always on hand to put to death some deed of the body that would bring guilt, sorrow, or personal tragedy. In the strength of the Spirit, the child of God can live his Heavenly Father's moral code. His commandments are not burdensome to his children, because "whatsoever is born of God overcometh the world" (1 John 5:4).

God succeeds in the moral development of his children because his method is that of love-oriented discipline. The Heavenly Father encourages his children to live in accord with his high moral precepts, and he gives them the wisdom and power to do so. When they succeed, he applauds and rewards them. When they fail, he corrects them. He may even chastise and rebuke them (Hebrews 12:6). But then he sets them on their feet, renewed and ready to begin again.

What a marvelous Father the children of God have! He doesn't tell them to look at his righteousness and imitate it, as an earthly father might. He actually puts his righteousness within them and then helps them to "work it out" in their daily lives! "For it is God which worketh in you both to will and to do of his good pleasure" (Philippians 2:13).

PART THREE

GOD AND HIS FAMILY

10
PROCLAIMING GOD AS FATHER

By informed estimates, more than half of America's children now may expect to live in a one-parent home during some part of their growing-up years. Since children usually go with their mothers when marriages break up, the absent parent in the one-parent family usually is the father.

But even in two-parent homes, the influence of the father can be damagingly deficient. In fact, the deficiency can be so great that the child would actually be better off in a reasonably calm one-parent home.

The shortcomings of father-absent homes, combined with those in which the father is present but deficient in the fulfillment of his roles in child development, produce an alarming situation. This poses the frightening prospect of a fatherless society, with all the social, economic, and political distortions such a condition would create.

The fast-developing fatherlessness of American society confronts evangelical Christianity with some serious questions:

Does the increasing fatherlessness of America merely constitute a problem, or is it also an opportunity for evangelism?

If it is an opportunity, how can evangelical Christianity deal with the obvious difficulties of introducing God as Father to people who have either no concept or a definitely negative concept of what a father is like?

OPPORTUNITY FOR EVANGELISM

I am personally convinced that born-again believers should consider the fatherless condition of many Americans as a choice opportunity for winning the lost to Jesus Christ.

It would be ridiculous, of course, to contend that the deterioration of marriage and the dissolution of the home are, in themselves, laudable developments. They are deplorable developments. God, who established these institutions, never intended for them to be disregarded or destroyed. What God hath joined together, let not man put asunder. The tearing apart of marriages and homes is the work of the devil, whose strategy is to counteract God's efforts to reveal himself to mankind.

But we know from the Scriptures that God is able to transmute evil into something good and beautiful. When Joseph's brothers sold him into slavery in Egypt, they meant it for evil. But as Joseph pointed out to them later, "God meant it unto good" (Genesis 50:20). He used Joseph's slavery to save the nation Israel during a famine that could have wiped them out.

Similarly, God can use America's increasing state of fatherlessness to help rather than hinder his outreach to the lost.

Social scientists see in the success of the cults, the popularity of literature pointing people to their "roots," and even in homosexuality and criminality a desperate search on the part of the masses for the father image they lack.

Fatherless America is in search of a father! What a glorious opportunity this presents for Christians to lead the nation to its Heavenly Father, the loving Creator and God of the universe! What a marvelous opportunity to say to lost America, "Here, my fatherless friends, here is your Heavenly Father, who has been searching for you longer than you've been searching for him!"

INTRODUCING GOD THE FATHER

Once evangelical Christians recognize the fatherlessness of America as an opportunity for evangelism, they can begin to cope with the question of how to introduce God to people who have an inadequate or negative father concept.

Jesus' role.
Christians must keep in mind that Jesus Christ reveals God as Father. If the fatherless are ever to know the Heavenly Father, they must be introduced to Jesus, his Son. Many Scriptures remind us of this important fact, and Jesus himself stated it a number of times. "All things are delivered to me of my Father: and no man knoweth who the Son is, but the Father; and who the Father is, but the Son, and he to whom the Son will reveal him" (Luke 10:22).

Anyone who comes to know the Father must do so through Jesus, the Son. No one else can reveal the Father because no one else even knows "who the Father is." Jesus alone must reveal the Father because Jesus alone *can* reveal the Father. No one will know the Father except the Son and those to whom the Son will reveal him.

Jesus also said, in John 14:6, "I am the way, the truth, and the life: no man cometh unto the Father, but by me." No one can go to the Father and have fellowship with him except through Jesus.

Many people today don't know what a father is like because they haven't had a satisfactory father model

99

in their homes. But even those who have been blessed with good earthly fathers can't know what the Heavenly Father is like except by observing what Jesus is like. "He that hath seen me hath seen the Father," Jesus told his disciples (John 14:9), and it would be as true to say that "he who hath *not* seen Jesus hath *not* seen the Father."

To truly understand what Jesus meant by these words, all we have to do is take a look at his life and his ministry.

In his teachings, Jesus revealed God to be a loving, spiritual Father, offering the benefits of membership in his family to all mankind. The Jews until that time had thought of God as an angry judge. But Jesus, revealing the true character of God, said, "Judge not" (Matthew 7:1) and told the woman caught in adultery, "Neither do I condemn thee" (John 8:11).

Jesus revealed through many of his statements, sermons, and parables that God is a forgiving Father. One of his best-known parables, the parable of the prodigal son, presents this very theme.

The prodigal son did nothing to merit his father's favor. In fact, he behaved in a rebellious manner that would have caused some earthly fathers to disown him. He despised his father's household, insisted on having his inheritance prematurely, and then turned his back on his home and his family and ran off to a foreign country. There he spent his money on parties and senseless pleasures. When he went broke, he dragged the family name into the filthy slime of some foreigner's hog pen. As he slopped the pigs one day, he caught a glimpse of his reflection in one of the mud puddles. Shocked by what he saw, he asked himself, "What is a man with a father like mine doing in a place like this?" Then and there he decided to go home.

On seeing this filthy wretch coming up the driveway, many an earthly father would have turned his back and said, "Go away—I don't even know you." But this father ran to meet his son, had the fatted calf slaughtered, and staged a big celebration over his homecoming.

What the lad had done wasn't the important thing to this father. The important thing was that he was his son, that he had been lost and missing but now had returned home.

That loving, forgiving Father whom Jesus was revealing in the parable was the Heavenly Father, the living God. And that is the Father whom Christians must keep in mind as they point fatherless Americans to Christ and urge them to find their true Father through him. It's easy for Christians who live sheltered lives in the family of God to forget this forgiving Father. It's easy for them, because they are not caught up in drugs or alcohol or crime, to become self-righteous and condemning in their attitudes toward the "prodigal sons" of the world. But we must remember how loathsome that prodigal son of the Bible must have been. And we must ask ourselves, "If the Father would receive such a sick, revolting creature as he, won't he also receive these unlovable wretches around me?"

In saying this, I don't mean that Christians should become soft on sin. I don't mean that we should excuse or condone evil. On the contrary, I believe we have to present a "hard gospel," a gospel that causes the lost and fatherless to be shaken into a realization of their sinful condition. We have to present God's message of repentance, the only path to salvation and righteousness.

The prodigal son returned to his father only when he "came to himself" (Luke 15:17), when he came to a realization of his hopeless condition. Americans need to become aware of their lost condition and turn to their Heavenly Father for forgiveness and salvation. The message of repentance is a double-edged sword. It teaches the lost not only that there is sin to be turned *from*, but also that there is a forgiving Father to turn *to*.

In presenting the gospel to fatherless America, we must expose both edges of that sword. To confront the fatherless with their sins and faults and stop there would be a grave mistake. It would dishonor God and leave most people in their lostness. To inform them only that God is a loving Father would be an equally tragic error. They wouldn't understand why they need a Father or what he could do for them. The fatherless American must know that he has sinned, that the wages of that sin is death, and that his Heavenly Father is the only One who can forgive him of that sin and give him eternal life.

And the message must state clearly that the only way to the Father is through Jesus Christ, who revealed him, first through his life and then through his death and resurrection.

The Holy Spirit's Role.
When we look at some of the unlovable, fatherless people around us, we're inclined to doubt they will ever turn to God. We just can't see them ever accepting Christ as Savior and coming to know God as their Heavenly Father. They seem too hardened in sin, too deaf to spiritual truth, too preoccupied with their pursuit of drugs, alcohol, sex, worldly pleasures, or false doctrines.

But here's the good news: Christians don't have to persuade these people to accept Christ. We don't have to talk them into recognizing God as their Heavenly Father or argue them into doing so. Even if we wanted to, we couldn't.

The Christian's role is simply to present the true gospel. It is every Christian's privilege to be a witness for Christ. Jesus told the disciples, "Ye shall be witnesses unto me" (Acts 1:8). Through the Apostle Paul, he said to those called as pastors or evangelists, "Preach the word" (2 Timothy 4:2).

When we have been faithful to our instructions to witness and preach, we must then trust the Holy Spirit to perform his work in those who will be saved. Jesus said, "No man can come unto me, except the Father which hath sent me draw him" (John 6:44). He also said, "And I, if I be lifted up from the earth [crucified], will draw all men unto me" (John 12:32).

As Christians, we're to proclaim to the world the truth of the crucified and resurrected Christ. But only the Father and Jesus himself can draw the lost to him. And the agent who does the work of the Father and the Son in drawing people to Christ is the Holy Spirit.

"But ye shall receive power, after that the Holy Ghost is come upon you: and ye shall be witnessses unto me both in Jerusalem, and in all Judea, and in Samaria, and unto the uttermost part of the earth" (Acts 1:8).

Christians should not witness except in the power of the Holy Spirit; that is, in a condition of being completely yielded to him and trusting in him to do his work in the heart of the one being witnessed to.

Jesus describes the work of the Holy Spirit in some detail in John 16:8-11: "And when he [the Holy Spirit] is come, he will reprove [convict] the world of sin, and of righteousness, and of judgment: Of sin, because they believe not on me; of righteousness, because I go to my Father, and ye see me no more; of judgment, because the prince of this world is judged."

As witnesses and preachers of the gospel, we are not the ones who bring sinners under conviction. We can't convict them of sin. We can't convince them that righteousness is available to them through Christ and a loving Heavenly Father. We can't convince them of the fact that their rejecting salvation, bought and paid for by the blood of Christ, will bring judgment, the everlasting wrath of God, and eternal punishment.

But, praise God, we don't have to convince them. That's the Holy Spirit's job. Our job is simply to place in the Spirit's hands the instrument he uses to get his job done—the living Word of God.

Hebrews 4:12 informs us of what an effective instrument God's Word becomes in the hands of the Holy Spirit: "For the word of God is quick, and powerful, and sharper than any two-edged sword, piercing even to the dividing asunder of soul and spirit, and of the joints and marrow, and is a discerner of the thoughts and intents of the heart."

Christians don't have to worry about the spiritual hardness of their lost friends, neighbors, and relatives. The Word of God, wielded by the Holy Spirit, is able to pierce the hardest defensive armor. It "discerns" the wickedness of the sinner's heart and reveals that wickedness to him.

People can't be saved until they are made to realize they are lost through this convicting work of the Holy Spirit. Countless thousands of times in my ministry, I've seen people come forward in tears to accept Christ. Many of them will say, "I was a churchgoer and I thought I was good, but I've just seen for the first time what a rotten sinner I am." That's the work of the Holy Spirit, using the Word of God to "reprove [convict] the world of sin."

The Christian's Role.
The reason many Americans are in effect fatherless is that we're living in a country where people don't know truth and don't know where to find it. Many churches and many Christians are failing in that when the fatherless go to them for the truth, they don't find it because Christians and churches who know the truth treat it as though it were unimportant. Many fatherless people see Christians and decide they don't want what they have—not because they're frightened away by their righteousness or Christlikeness, but because they're turned off by their hypocrisy.

The false prophets and cults tell people that if they want to be part of their movements, they have to give all, they have to give up everything. But many churches and many Christians have been telling people they can become Christians and not give God anything. They teach, with their watered down gospel and unrepentant life-styles, that people can become Christians and go on living just as they are.

That's not the true gospel. Jesus said, "If any man will come after me, let him deny himself, and take up his cross daily, and follow me" (Luke 9:23). In Matthew 16:25, 26 he said, "For whosoever will save his life shall lose it: and whosoever will lose his life for my sake shall find it. For what is a man profited, if he shall gain the whole world, and lose his own soul? or what shall a man give in exchange for his soul?"

In New Testament days, many Christians lost their lives when they came to Christ. They were slaughtered like sheep, not because they called themselves Christians, but because they had given their all to Christ. And having given their all to Christ, they refused to worship Caesar.

The false gospel preached by many churches and proclaimed by many Christians in America today is that people can worship both God and Caesar. That's a lie. Being a Christian in affluent America means the same as it meant in New Testament Rome. It means denying self. It means giving all to Christ.

Many remain fatherless in America because Christians have cheapened the gospel, abandoned the message of repentance, and geared their church services to making people comfortable despite their unrepentant and unrighteous condition.

Diluting the gospel in preaching and witnessing results in powerless Christians and stagnant churches. I can understand why America's fatherless pass by churches sealed off from the lost world by their stained glass windows and filled with people who look like they have been embalmed. Many unsaved say they have rejected Christianity because the churches they have seen resemble country clubs more than centers of compassion and concern.

When Jesus described what the Christian witness should be like he said, "Verily, verily, I say unto you, He that believeth on me, the works that I do shall he do also; and greater works than these shall he do. . ." (John 14:12).

That's the kind of Christian whose witness is going to turn the fatherless to their Heavenly Father—the kind who is so committed to Christ that he does the works that Christ did in the world, the kind who is so filled with the Holy Spirit that the world sees Jesus Christ in his life.

When Jesus described the church he would build, he

visualized it as a force of such vibrance and power that the gates of hell itself would tremble and fall in its path (Matthew 16:18). That's the kind of church that will draw the fatherless to Christ and introduce them to their Heavenly Father through him.

To have that kind of Christian and that kind of church, those who name Christ as their Savior must realize that they can't worship God and Caesar. They must realize that to follow Christ, they must repent. They must give up everything for the cause of leading the fatherless to the Father.

Deuteronomy 26:12, 13 says, "When thou hast made an end of tithing all the tithes of thine increase the third year . . . and hast given it unto the Levite, the stranger, the fatherless, and the widow . . . Then thou shalt say before the Lord thy God, I have brought away the hallowed things out of mine house, and also have given them unto the Levite, and unto the stranger, to the fatherless, and to the widow. . . ."

When Christians have given up all for Christ, when they have renounced the world, then they will have "hallowed things" to give to the fatherless. They will have Spirit-filled lives that will draw people to the Heavenly Father.

"If any man love the world, the love of the Father is not in him" (1 John 2:15). The fatherless will not look for the Heavenly Father in those who love the world and therefore do not have the love of the Father in them.

11

A NEW FAMILY AND FUTURE

Social scientists are discovering what many thoughtful Christians have already known—God established the family for more than one purpose. It was not to be merely a training school for earthly living and a building block for society. It was also to provide a glimpse of life in the spiritual family of God.

Ideally, the natural family should begin to meet the need every human being has for parents and intimate associations with other people. It also should prepare people as they grow up to participate constructively in the larger, spiritual family headed by the Heavenly Father.

However, as already discussed, the Heavenly Father is able to more than fulfill all the roles of an earthly father. The lack of a satisfactory father image in the home need not permanently distort personality development. God the Father overcomes psychological deficiencies and corrects flaws or inadequacies in development through his supernatural power and wisdom.

To perform his corrective socialization, the Heavenly Father takes those who have become his children through faith in Jesus Christ and places them in the stimulating environment of the family of God, his church. The Apostle Paul describes the change that occurs: "Do not be deceived; neither fornicators, nor idolaters, nor adulterers, nor effeminate, nor homosexuals, nor thieves, nor the covetous, nor drunkards, nor revilers, nor swindlers, shall inherit the kingdom of God. And such were some of you; but you were washed, but you were sanctified, but you were justified in the name of the Lord Jesus Christ, and in the Spirit of our God" (1 Corinthians 6:9-11, *New American Standard Bible*).

The earliest Christians displayed many developmental defects in their lives before entering God's family. Some were trying to find the answers to their problems in sexual indulgence, alcohol, worldly riches and pleasures, and even in homosexuality. Yet Paul says that in receiving God as Father and being brought into his family they were cleansed, changed, and set apart for a new life-style.

In his new spiritual family, the person who has turned to the Heavenly Father has developmental advantages he could never experience in any earthly family. The family of God is a huge family in which the relationships with the Father and other family members are closer than those of the natural family. All have the same Father, for there is "one God and Father of all, who is above all, and through all, and in you all" (Ephesians 4:6). All share the same spiritual identity and in a very real sense are part of one another. They are one with each other and with the Father, just as Jesus Christ and the Father are one (John 17:22).

Paul explains in his heartwarming passage in Romans 8 something of what it means to become a member of God's family. Beginning in verse 15, he reveals that the method of entrance into the family of God is by adoption. Paul stresses that when God makes an adoption, the child has every right to regard God as his Father in the full sense of the word. He notes that the Holy Spirit, who is given at the time of adoption, assures each family member that he is a child of God. Being a child adopted into God's family makes the child a "joint-heir" with Christ, sharing equally with him all the blessings and privileges of God's kingdom (verse 17).

Membership in the family of God carries many important responsibilites for the child of God. The basic responsibility, however, is simply to believe in the Father and trust him as he fulfills his father role in developing the child's spiritual maturity.

Paul warns, in verse 17, that the Father's work in the life of the child can result in suffering. The suffering God permits, however, is not meant to injure the child but to help him progress toward the goal set for him by his Heavenly Father. That goal, as revealed by Paul, is nothing short of the spiritual maturity exhibited by Jesus Christ. "For whom he [God] did foreknow, he also did predestinate to be conformed to the image of his Son, that he [Jesus] might be the firstborn among many brethren" (Romans 8:29).

The standards in a family in which God is the Father and Jesus Christ the first-born Son are, of course, quite high. They are so high, in fact, that they are beyond the reach of human wisdom and energy. But, thank God, they are attainable in the power of God the Father. Paul, in his letter to the Philippians, prescribes the proper attitude for the child of God: "Being confident of this very thing, that he which hath begun a good work in you will perform it until the day of Jesus Christ" (1:6).

If you are a child of God, it is God the Father who has begun a good work in you. He began it when he gave you spiritual birth and adopted you into his family. And you can be confident that your Heavenly Father, having begun his work in you, will continue it until Jesus returns to take you with him to your heavenly home.

The important point for you to remember as a child of God is that your part is not to try to do the corrective, developmental work that needs to be done in your life. Your part is simply to submit yourself to God as you would to a loving physician whom you trust implicitly. It is the Father who does the work. For those who enter the family of God and humbly submit to the Father, one of the immediate and most precious blessings is a sense of peace. "Peace I leave with you, my peace I give unto you: not as the world giveth, give I unto you," Jesus said (John 14:27).

Life for the fatherless of this world is characterized by restlessness—a vague feeling of dissatisfaction, of being constantly in search of some lacking quality or element. Such restlessness is understandable, in view of the universal need for a father and a family. But it vanishes when God is recognized as Father and his church as the long-sought family. When the source of dissatisfaction is removed, the search is ended. "And the peace of God, which passeth all understanding, shall keep your hearts and minds through Christ Jesus" (Philippians 4:7).

In addition to a father and a family, sociologists and psychologists find that people need assurance with regard to the future. They need to be secure about their destiny, to know where they are headed.

Having God as Father fulfills that need with a certainty and splendor that the human mind can't begin to imagine. Because of our limited ability to envision a future so magnificent, even the Bible provides only dim outlines of the tomorrow that awaits every child of God. What the Scriptures do reveal, though, is so exciting and reassuring that it offers the child of God a security and contentment unknown to the lost and fatherless.

The principal characteristics of the future of which God's children are assured include its purity, its permanence, and the certainty of the presence of those to whom it is promised. These characteristics are set forth by the Apostle Peter: "Blessed be the God and Father of our Lord Jesus Christ, which according to his abundant mercy hath begotten us again unto a lively hope by the resurrection of Jesus Christ from the dead, to an inheritance incorruptible, and undefiled, and that fadeth not away, reserved in heaven for you, who are kept by the power of God through faith unto salvation ready to be revealed in the last time" (1 Peter 1:3-5).

If you are a child of God, your future is pure—"incorruptible, and undefiled." It is permanent—it "fadeth not away, but is reserved in heaven for you." And because you are "kept by the power of God," you will be delivered safe to your inherited estate and will be able to enjoy it forever.

Little wonder that Peter's next words were, "Wherein ye greatly rejoice. . . ." This is the future all mankind yearns for, consciously or unconsciously. Yet it is promised only to the children of God, those who come to know him as Father through faith in Jesus Christ. How could they help but rejoice?

3067   3